Key Stage 3 Science

Spectrum

Physics

Andy Cooke

Jean Martin

CAMBRIDGE
UNIVERSITY PRESS

Series editors	Andy Cooke
	Jean Martin
Consultant	Sam Ellis
Authors	Andy Cooke
	Sam Ellis
	David Glover
	Jean Martin
	Janet McKechnie
	Chris Ram
	Nicky Thomas

CAMBRIDGE UNIVERSITY PRESS
Cambridge, New York, Melbourne, Madrid, Cape Town, Singapore, São Paulo

Cambridge University Press
The Edinburgh Building, Cambridge CB2 2RU, UK

www.cambridge.org
Information on this title: www.cambridge.org/9780521549233

First published 2004
Reprinted 2004, 2006

Printed in Italy by G. Canale & C. S.p.A.

A catalogue record for this publication is available from the British Library

ISBN-13 978-0-521-54923-3 paperback
ISBN-10 0-521-54923-X paperback

Material in this book was previously published in *Spectrum Year 7 Class Book*
(pp. 105–162), *Spectrum Year 8 Class Book* (pp. 97–146) and *Spectrum Year 9 Class
Book* (pp. 107–158).

Cover design by Blue Pig Design Co
Page make-up and illustration by Hardlines Ltd, Charlbury, Oxford

Contents

About *Spectrum* Physics

This *Spectrum* Class Book covers what you will learn about science and scientists in Key Stage 3 physics. It is split into twelve **Units**. Each Unit starts with a page like this:

A Unit code.

9K

Speeding up

A Unit title.

KEY WORDS
speed
unit
acceleration

A list of **key words** that are important for you to understand.

Each Unit is split into **Topics** that cover one part of what you need to know.

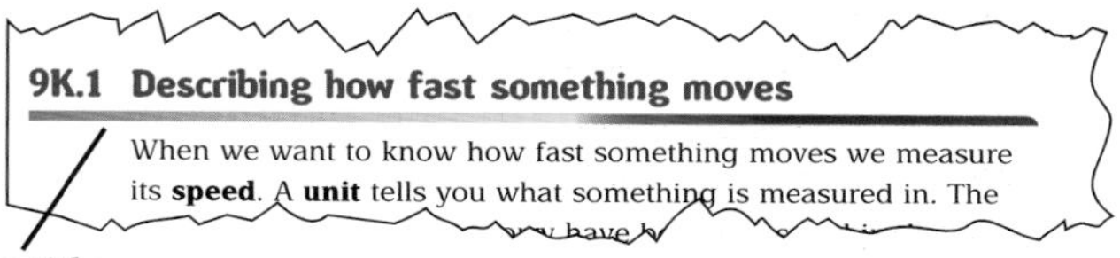

9K.1 Describing how fast something moves

When we want to know how fast something moves we measure its **speed**. A **unit** tells you what something is measured in. The

A Topic title.

A section title.

Each Topic has **sections** describing one important idea or group of ideas that are important for you to understand.

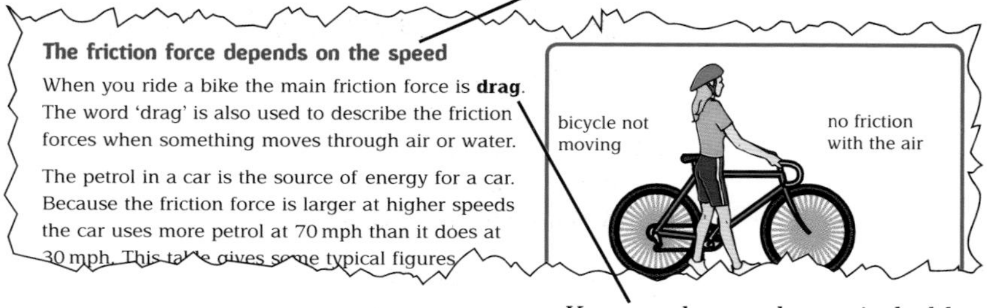

The friction force depends on the speed

When you ride a bike the main friction force is **drag**. The word 'drag' is also used to describe the friction forces when something moves through air or water.

The petrol in a car is the source of energy for a car. Because the friction force is larger at higher speeds the car uses more petrol at 70 mph than it does at 30 mph. This table gives some typical figures

bicycle not moving

no friction with the air

Key words are shown in bold.

Each Unit finishes with a **summary** of key words and ideas so you can see what you have learnt.

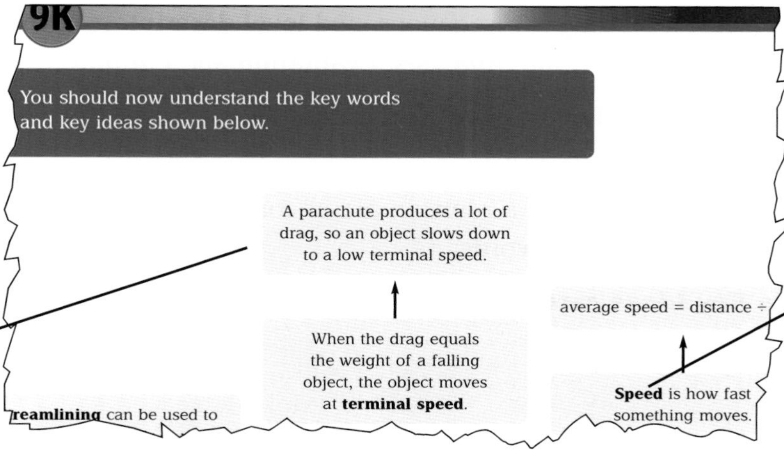

9K

You should now understand the key words and key ideas shown below.

A parachute produces a lot of drag, so an object slows down to a low terminal speed.

An important idea.

When the drag equals the weight of a falling object, the object moves at **terminal speed**.

average speed = distance ÷

A key word.

Speed is how fast something moves.

reamlining can be used to

Icons

 Telling you where to look in the Class Book to help with activities.

 Asking questions about what you have just learnt.

 Asking questions that help you think about what you have just learnt.

 Asking questions that might need some research to answer.

At the end of the book

At the end of the book you will find:

- pages 161 to 168 to help you with **scientific investigations**;

- a **glossary/index** to help you look up words and find out their meanings.

Other components of *Spectrum*

Your teacher has other components of *Spectrum Physics* that they can use to help you learn. They have:

- a **Teacher file CD-ROM** full of information for them and lots of activities of different kinds for you. The activities are split into three levels: **support**, **main** and **extension**. Some of the activities are **suitable for homework**.

Also available by year:

- an **assessment CD-ROM** with an **analysis tool**. The CD-ROM has **multiple choice tests** to find out what you know before you start a Unit and for you to do during or after a Unit. It also has some end of year **SAT-style tests**.

And free on the web available at www.cambridge.org/spectrum:

- general guidance documents on aspects of the Science Framework;

- **investigation checklists**, **investigation sheets** – writing frames to help with structuring investigations, and **level descriptors** covering **Planning**, **Observation**, **Analysis**, **Evaluation** and **Communication**;

- **mapping grids** for the **Five Key Ideas**, **Numeracy**, **Literacy**, **ICT**, **Citizenship** and **Sc1**;

- **flash cards** for use as a revision aid or for card chases using the Years 7, 8 and 9 key words;

- **Five Key Ideas cards** for use as a revision aid and to build giant concept maps.

Energy resources

In this unit we shall be studying what energy is and how we use it.

71.1   Energy and fuels

Energy is one of the big ideas in science. It is so important that it has its own unit, **joules**. We measure energy in joules.

What energy is

Anything that involves energy change can be called work. Nothing can happen without energy making it happen.

The microwave oven needs energy to cook.

The cheetah needs energy to run.

The rocket needs energy to take off.

The plant needs energy to grow.

To do work energy must change in some way. It can:

● move from one place to another – this is called energy <u>transfer</u>;

● change from one type of energy to another – this is called <u>transformation</u>.

KEY WORDS

energy
joules
gravitational potential
chemical
kinetic
heat
light
elastic potential
electrical
sound
engine
Bunsen burner
fossil fuel
coal
mineral oil
natural gas
non-renewable
renewable
wind
tidal
solar
wave
hydro-electric
geothermal
biomass

1   What is meant by energy?

2   What must energy do to make things happen?

3   Make a list of <u>six</u> things that you think need energy to make them happen or work.

There are different types of energy

We are surrounded by different types of energy. Once you know what they are, you can spot them everywhere.

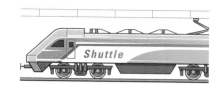

Gravitational potential energy is stored in things which are high up.

Fuels store **chemical energy**.

A moving object has **kinetic energy**.

Heat energy is given out by hot objects.

Light energy is given out by luminous objects.

Elastic potential energy is stored in things which are squashed or stretched.

Electrical energy is the energy carried by electricity.

Sound energy is given out by loudspeakers.

 4 Name the eight types of energy.

 5 List any types of energy that are present in your classroom.

Making things happen

We know that energy needs to change from one type to another to make things happen. We can show some of these changes using an energy transformation diagram. The picture shows an example:

 6 What type of energy does a kettle transform electrical energy into?

 7 What useful energy does a bulb transform electrical energy into?

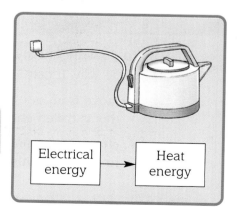

Electrical energy → Heat energy

Useful fuels

Fuels have chemical energy stored in them. We burn fuels to release this stored energy as heat. We use the energy to make lots of useful things happen.

- Most of our electrical energy comes from burning fuels in power stations. This is then transformed into electrical energy by generators.

- In the science laboratory you will use a Bunsen burner. This burns methane or propane gas to release heat energy.

In everyday life we use lots of different fuels to do different jobs. In a car this fuel is usually petrol or diesel. It burns inside the **engine**.

 8 Look at the five pictures showing different fuels being used. Then, list <u>five</u> common fuels.

 9 What fuel can be used instead of petrol and diesel?

10 Which fuel was used to light street lights in the 19th century?

We burn fuels to do jobs for us. These jobs mainly fall into one of four categories: transport, heating, cooking and making electricity.

Oil is used to heat schools.

Aircraft use aviation fuel.

Gas is used to cook.

Coal is used to generate electricity.

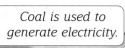

 11 What are the <u>four</u> main categories of uses for fuels?

 12 Which fuels can be used to heat our homes ?

13 Name a fuel (other than the one shown in the picture) that can be used in a power station.

Using a Bunsen burner safely

The **Bunsen burner** was invented in 1855 by a German chemist called Robert Bunsen. It burns methane or propane to produce a hot flame. To use it safely, you must follow these important safety rules:

Step 1: Safety goggles (eye protection) must be worn all the time.

Step 2: Long hair must be tied back. All loose clothing must be tucked in.

Step 3: The Bunsen burner should be placed on the middle of a heatproof mat, in the middle of your bench. Securely attach the side tube to the gas tap.

Step 4: Light the Bunsen burner with the air hole closed, at arm's length using a lighted splint. Do not turn on the gas until the lighted splint is above the barrel of the Bunsen burner.

It is important that you follow the other important lab rules as well, such as never running in a lab.

The size of the flame is controlled using the gas tap. The type of flame is controlled by opening and closing the air hole.

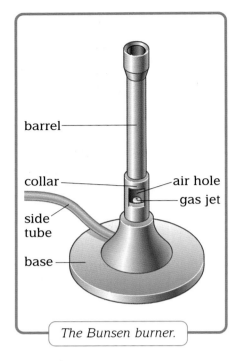

The Bunsen burner.

14 Who invented the Bunsen burner?

15 How do you control the type of flame?

16 The unit for energy is the joule. Try and find out as much as you can about James Joule. Try making a time-line of his life or write a short biography.

Bunsen burner flames.

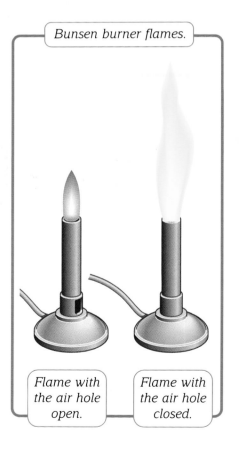

Flame with the air hole open.

Flame with the air hole closed.

71.2 Fossil fuels

Fossil fuels, like **coal**, **mineral oil** and **natural gas** come from plants and animals that died millions of years ago. They are very important to us as fuels and for making materials like plastics.

Fossil fuels are made from dead plants and animals

Fossil fuels were made millions of years ago from the remains of dead plants and animals. You can see the fossilised remains of plants in coal.

The piece of coal has the fossilised remains of a plant in it.

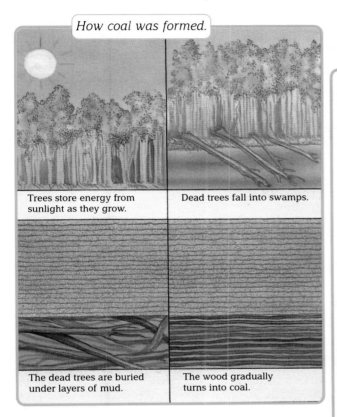

How coal was formed.

Trees store energy from sunlight as they grow.

Dead trees fall into swamps.

The dead trees are buried under layers of mud.

The wood gradually turns into coal.

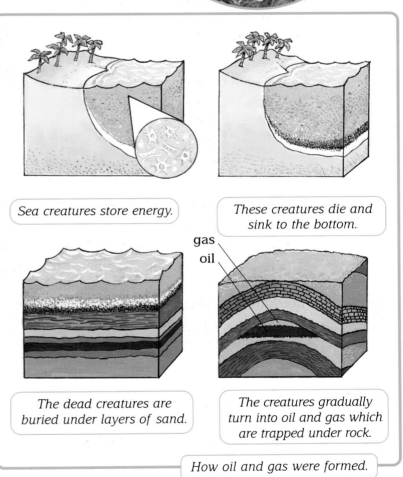

Sea creatures store energy.

These creatures die and sink to the bottom.

gas
oil

The dead creatures are buried under layers of sand.

The creatures gradually turn into oil and gas which are trapped under rock.

How oil and gas were formed.

1 Where does the chemical energy in fossil fuels come from?

2 How do oil and gas become trapped? How do we get at them?

Fossil fuels will run out

All the fossil fuels take many millions of years to form. We are using them up far faster than they are being replaced. Fossil fuels are **non-renewable**. This means that one day they will run out. It is estimated that we have enough coal to last 300 years, enough gas to last 60 years and enough oil to last 40 years. These estimates assume that we will keep using them at the same rate we do today and that no more fossil fuels will be discovered.

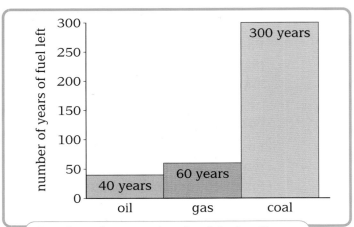

Bar chart showing when fossil fuels will run out based on current rates of consumption of known world reserves.

3 Fossil fuels are non-renewable. What does this mean?

4 How old will you be when oil runs out, if oil runs out in the time shown in the bar chart?

5 How long do you think fossil fuels will actually last? State your reasons.

How we use fossil fuels is always changing

The Industrial Revolution happened in Britain before anywhere else. People started to work in large factories and use lots of machines. The fuel they used was coal. Britain had plenty of coal, underground. Men, women and children worked in dark, dirty and dangerous coal mines, to get it. The picture shows this.

Today, in Britain, coal has become less popular. Natural gas, which comes from the North Sea, is being used more and more, because it burns more cleanly.

Mineral oil has become increasingly popular, since it was first drilled for in Pennsylvania, USA, in 1859. This is because of the ever increasing numbers of cars and other vehicles across the world. In the future, fossil fuel use is likely to increase as more and more countries become industrialised.

6 Why is coal being used less and less in Britain today?

7 Why is the use of fossil fuels likely to increase across the world, despite the pollution it causes?

We use fossil fuels to make most of our electricity

We need electricity for every part of our lives, at home and at work. Most of our electrical energy is transformed from the chemical energy in fuels. The table shows advantages and disadvantages of different fossil fuels used to make electricity.

Fossil fuels	Advantages	Disadvantages
Coal, mineral oil and natural gas	Reliable, concentrated forms of energy	Need to be transported and stored; burning them contributes to global warming
Coal	Plentiful supply	Burning it contributes to acid rain
Mineral oil	Can transport it in pipes	Bad sea pollution possible from oil spills from tankers
Natural gas	Burns more cleanly than others	Difficult to drill for

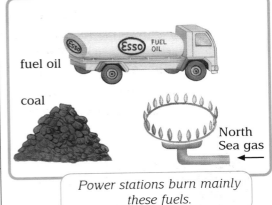

fuel oil

coal

North Sea gas

Power stations burn mainly these fuels.

8 Where does most of our electrical energy come from?

9 What is an advantage of using natural gas to produce electricity?

10 What is a disadvantage of using coal to produce electricity?

It is important to save fuels

It is important to save fossil fuels because they are running out and because burning them is the main cause of air pollution. This air pollution is causing problems such as global warming, acid rain and smog. Fuels can be saved by expanding the use of renewable energy resources, which you will find out about next, and by using machines that need less energy to do the same job, such as energy efficient light bulbs.

Gases from car exhausts cause air pollution.

11 What are the <u>two</u> reasons why it is important to save fuels?

12 Why does the cyclist in the picture need to wear an air filter?

Lots of countries also generate electricity in nuclear power stations. These generate a lot of heat energy that then gets converted into electricity. Nuclear reactors give out dangerous radiation. So thick walls are built around them to protect us.

13 Find out what happened at the Chernobyl nuclear power station in 1986. It has made a lot of people worry about nuclear power stations.

71.3 Renewable energy resources

Fossil fuels will run out one day. We say they are non-renewable. They also cause pollution. This has led to the development of alternatives to fossil fuels. Many of these alternatives are **renewable** energy resources. They will never run out.

Renewable energy resources won't run out

In the future, renewable energy resources will play a bigger role. Renewable energy resources, such as **wind** energy and **tidal** energy, will last almost for ever. As we use them, they are naturally topped up by a fresh supply.

The Sun will keep on shining for about 5 billion more years.

So **solar** energy is a renewable energy resource.

?
1   How long will renewable energy resources last?
2   Name a renewable energy resource.

Most renewable energy resources depend on the Sun

The diagrams show how the **wind**, a **wave** on the sea and hydro-electric power stations get their energy from the Sun.

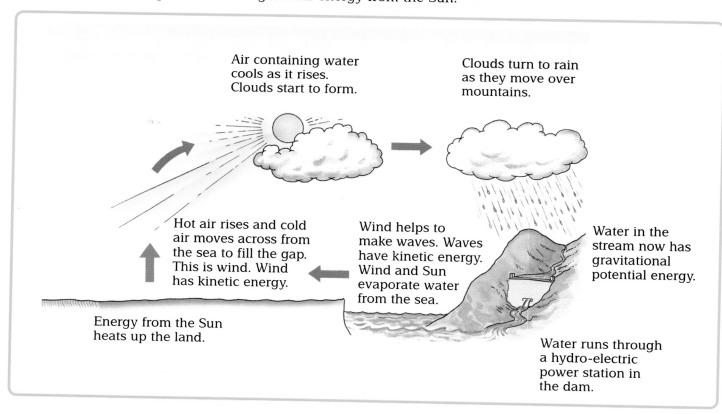

Air containing water cools as it rises. Clouds start to form.

Clouds turn to rain as they move over mountains.

Hot air rises and cold air moves across from the sea to fill the gap. This is wind. Wind has kinetic energy.

Wind helps to make waves. Waves have kinetic energy. Wind and Sun evaporate water from the sea.

Water in the stream now has gravitational potential energy.

Energy from the Sun heats up the land.

Water runs through a hydro-electric power station in the dam.

Not all renewable energy resources depend on the Sun. Tidal energy comes from the gravitational pull of the Moon (and the Sun). **Geothermal** energy comes from the heat energy in hot rocks deep underground.

3 Name <u>two</u> renewable energy resources that depend on the Sun.

4 Name <u>two</u> renewable energy resources that don't depend on the Sun.

5 Explain how energy from the Sun makes the wind blow.

6 Explain why hydro-electric energy comes from the Sun.

Trees need energy from the Sun to grow. This energy is stored in all the material from which the plant is made, including the wood. It is known as **biomass** energy.

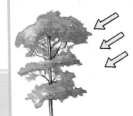

Energy is transferred to trees by sunlight. Trees store this energy as they grow. So trees are stores of chemical energy. You can burn the wood as a fuel.

7 Explain what biomass energy is.

8 How can that energy be released from wood?

9 Look at the table on pages 10–11. What is a disadvantage of tidal energy?

10 What is an advantage of all renewable energy resources?

11 Wood could be described as both renewable and non-renewable. Explain why.

There are lots of renewable energy resources

It is difficult to work out how expensive renewable energy resources really are. Read the table to find out about them.

Name of renewable energy resource	Solar energy	Wind energy	Tidal energy
Ultimate source of energy	The Sun	The Sun	Moon's gravitational pull
How it is used	Solar cells turn the Sun's energy directly into electricity. Solar panels on roofs convert solar energy into heat energy.	The kinetic energy of the wind is used to turn large turbines, which drive generators which convert the kinetic energy into electricity.	A barrier called a barrage is built across the estuary (tidal mouth of a river). This acts as a dam. As water is brought in by the tides it gets trapped in the estuary. As this trapped water returns to the sea, it drives turbines in the barrage, which in turn drive generators.
An advantage	Solar cells are useful for portable devices like radios.	Technology well developed	No pollution
A disadvantage	Still quite expensive	Wind turbines look ugly	Building cost is very large.
	solar energy array of solar cells solar energy solar panel	w i n d → turbine → generator The wind makes the turbine turn. This drives the generator.	When the barrage is built the mud flats in the estuary are flooded all the time.

Hydro-electricity	Biomass energy	Wave energy	Geothermal energy
Gravitational potential energy	The Sun	The Sun	Heat energy in hot rocks deep underground
Water trapped behind a dam is used to make electricity, by letting water flow downhill.	Biomass is the energy stored in plant material like wood. There are lots of ways of releasing this energy. For example, sugar from sugar cane can be converted into alcohol, which can then be used as a fuel for cars.	The up-and-down movement of sea water can be used to make electricity.	Cold water is pumped deep underground, in a suitable place. It comes back up as steam. The energy in the steam is used to make electricity.
No pollution	Using biomass energy more means using fossil fuels less.	No pollution	Low levels of general pollution.
Areas of land may be flooded.	Burning releases carbon dioxide.	Corrosion of machinery by the salty water	Sulphurous smell can be a problem locally.
		Water moves up and down inside the tube. This drives air through the turbine.	

71.4 Living things and energy

All living things, including us, use energy. All activity, including just being alive, needs energy. Food is the energy resource that animals and plants need to live and do things.

We need energy from food for everything we do

Different activities need different amounts of energy. If you lift an apple up 1 m, it uses 1 J of energy. A joule isn't much energy at all, so sometimes the kilojoule is used. 1 kilojoule is the same as 1000 joules. The pictures show how much energy different activities use every minute.

Jogging needs 60 kilojoules of energy for every minute you jog.

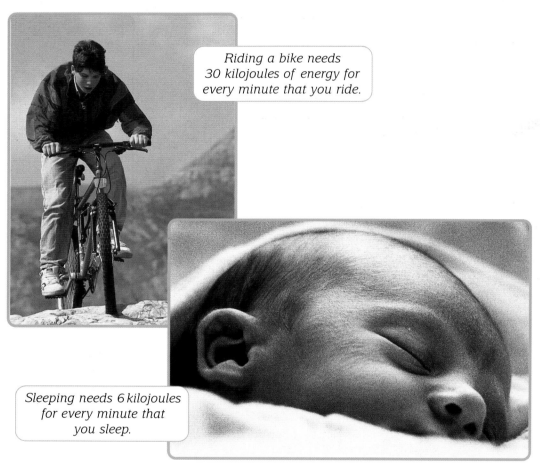

Riding a bike needs 30 kilojoules of energy for every minute that you ride.

Sleeping needs 6 kilojoules for every minute that you sleep.

Walking needs 20 kilojoules for every minute you are strolling along.

1 Which of the four activities needs the least energy?

2 Can you think of any other things that might affect the amount of energy a person needs?

Animals eat food to get their energy

Animals need to eat food to get energy. If you look on food labels you can see that there is an old unit for energy used as well. This is called the kilocalorie (kcal). This is just like having two different units for length: centimetres and inches. Either unit tells you how much chemical energy is stored in food.

Nutrition labels

Food a

NUTRITION INFORMATION
100 g provides: Energy 1500 kJ / 370 kcal. Protein 4.5 g. Carbohydrate 67 g. (of which sugars 29 g) (starch 33 g). Fat 10 g (of which saturates 2 g). Fibre 3 g. Sodium 0.3 g. Vitamins: Thiamin B_1 1 mg (70%). Riboflavin B_2 1.1 mg (70%). Niacin 12 mg (70%). Vitamin B_6 1.4 mg (70%). Folic Acid 135 µg (70%). Vitamin B_{12} 0.7 µg (70%). Minerals: Calcium 540 mg (70%). Iron 6.4 mg (45%).

Food b

NUTRITION INFORMATION	PER PIECE	PER 100 g
ENERGY:	1180 kJ / 281 kcal	1885 kJ / 449 kcal
PROTEIN:	2.6 g	4.2 g
CARBOHYDRATE:	43.1 g	69.0 g
FAT:	10.9 g	17.4 g

3 Which of the two foods has more energy per 100 g?

4 What type of energy is stored in food?

The physicist John Tyndall worked out that the energy he needed to climb a mountain called the Matterhorn was contained in a ham sandwich, so that was all the food he took with him!

The energy in food comes from the Sun

Like all living things, plants need food to live and grow. Unlike animals, they make their own food using the energy in sunlight. Patrick eats meat, which comes from an animal. The animal he eats got its energy in the first place from plants. The plants got their energy to live and grow from the Sun. So, all our food energy resources originally came from the Sun.

The potato plant uses the energy in sunlight to make its food.

 energy energy energy

5 Where do plants get the energy from to make their food?

6 How are animals and plants different, in terms of the food they need?

7 Why is it more energy efficient to eat plants rather than animals?

You should now know the meaning of these words:

fossil fuel	mineral oil	hydro-electric	heat
Bunsen burner	natural gas	solar	sound
renewable	biomass	wave	light
non-renewable	wind	chemical	gravitational potential
joules	geothermal	kinetic	elastic potential
coal	tidal	electrical	engine

You should also have an understanding of these key ideas:

- **Energy** is the ability to do work. It is measured in **joules**.

- There are different types of energy such as **kinetic** energy and **heat** energy.

- Fuels are very important in our lives. We have many different fuels that we use.

- The energy that fuels release is useful for transport, heating, cooking and making electricity.

- The **Bunsen burner** is used in the school laboratory to release energy for doing experiments. It is important to follow the safety rules when using it.

- **Fossil fuels** are made from dead plants and animals. They formed over millions of years.

- Fossil fuels will run out. They are **non-renewable**.

- We use fossil fuels to make most of our electricity.

- It is important to save fuels because they are running out and because burning them causes air pollution.

- **Renewable** energy resources such as **wind** energy won't run out as long as the Sun keeps shining.

- Most renewable energy resources depend on the Sun.

- There are lots of renewable energy resources, such as **geothermal** energy and **solar** energy.

- Renewable energy resources do not cause air pollution.

- Animals eat food to get their energy. The energy in food is measured in kilojoules or kilocalories.

- Activities that we do all need energy. We get the energy we need from the chemical energy in food.

- Plants make food using the energy in sunlight.

- All the energy in food ultimately comes from the Sun.

- We need to balance the energy in our diet.

Electrical circuits

In this unit we shall be finding out how electrical circuits work and how electricity can be used safely in the home.

7J.1 How electrical circuits work

We use electrical devices in our everyday lives, but we often don't think about how they are put together. We are going to study how to connect electrical components together to make a **circuit** which works.

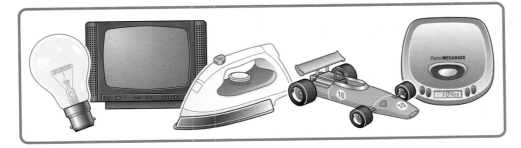

Making a circuit

Electricity will only flow when a circuit is complete. These diagrams show four attempts at making a **bulb** light up. Only one will work.

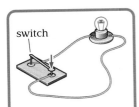

switch

There is no source of energy to make the electricity flow, so the bulb will not light up.

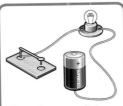

There is a gap. It is not a complete circuit, so the electricity cannot flow around.

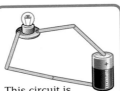

This circuit is connected using wood. Wood does not let electricity flow through it. Wood is not a conductor.

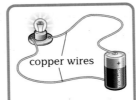

copper wires

This is a complete circuit, electricity can flow and the bulb will light up.

1   Describe how you would need to connect a battery, bulb and switch so that the bulb lights up. Draw a picture of this.

2   What sort of material would you need to use to make leads to connect an electrical circuit?

Using a switch

Sometimes we need to be able to break the circuit to stop the electricity flowing. We can do this by using a **switch**. When a switch is <u>closed</u> the circuit is complete and electricity can flow. When the switch is <u>open</u> the circuit is not complete so electricity cannot flow. We often say that we 'switch something on'. This means that a switch is closed to make a circuit.

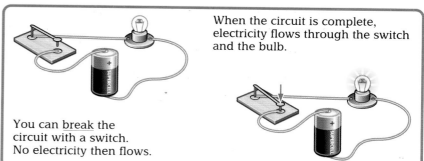

When the circuit is complete, electricity flows through the switch and the bulb.

You can <u>break</u> the circuit with a switch. No electricity then flows.

A torch is a device that contains a simple circuit. A battery is connected to a switch and a bulb. When the torch is needed the switch can be closed so that the bulb lights up. When the torch is not needed, the switch can be opened to prevent the battery running down.

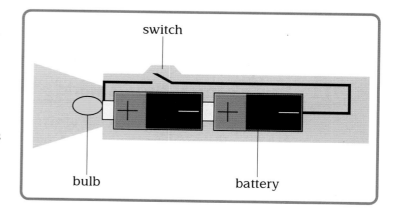

switch

bulb

battery

3 How does a switch turn off the bulb in a torch?

4 When we 'switch an appliance on' what change are we making to the circuit?

5 Why do you need a switch in a torch?

Drawing a circuit

It is useful to have a quick way of drawing the components in a circuit. Instead of drawing pictures we can draw symbols to represent the components. It is important to remember these symbols and use them when drawing your circuits.

You will find out about other symbols later in the unit.

Component	Symbol
Cell	—————┤├——————
Battery	————┤├—┤├————
Connection	————————————
Open switch	——————o⟋ o————
Closed switch	——————o—o————
Bulb	——————⊗——————

We can now use these symbols to draw circuit diagrams.

This is the circuit diagram for the torch.

Look carefully at these four circuit pictures and use them to answer questions 6 and 7.

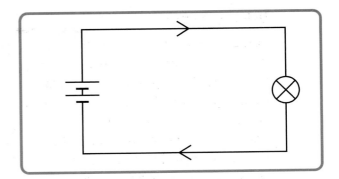

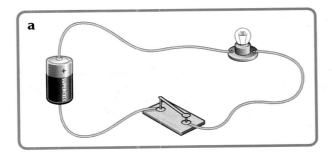

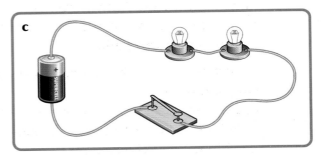

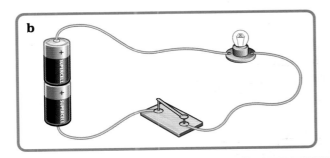

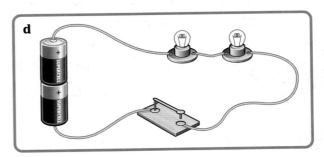

6   Draw circuit diagrams for each of the four circuits.

7   **a** In which of these circuits will the bulb not light up?

   b In which of these circuits <u>do you think</u> the bulb or bulbs will be brightest?

8   In some houses the light on the landing can be switched on upstairs or downstairs. Either design or research a circuit which could use two switches to operate one bulb. The bulb must light up when you close one switch or the other, not both.

7J.2 Inside a circuit

We are now going to look at what is happening inside a circuit once it is connected up. We are also going to find out how to change the brightness of a bulb in a circuit.

Series circuits

In a **series** circuit all components are connected in one loop. This diagram shows a circuit with two bulbs in series.

In this circuit there is only one path around the circuit for the electricity to follow, so all the electricity flows through all the components in the circuit. Bulbs are not the only components that can be connected in series. You need to choose the components for the job you want the circuit to perform.

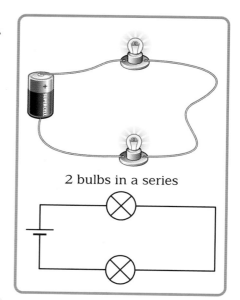

2 bulbs in a series

1   What is a series circuit?

2   What power supply is used in the circuit above?

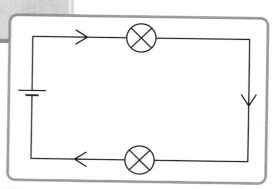

Electric current

In a complete circuit we say that there is an electric **current** which flows around the circuit. We say that this current flows from the positive side of the **power supply**, around the circuit and back to the negative side of the power supply.

3   Which way does the electric current flow around a circuit?

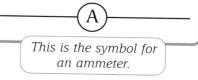

This is the symbol for an ammeter.

We can measure the electric current in any circuit by using an **ammeter**. An ammeter tells us the value of the current in amperes (**amps** or 'A' for short). This picture shows an ammeter showing a reading of 0.15 A.

When we use an ammeter in a circuit we connect it in series with the other components. This means that all of the current flows through the ammeter. The diagram shows how the ammeter should be connected.

4   What unit do we use to measure the electric current?

5   Describe how an ammeter should be connected in a circuit.

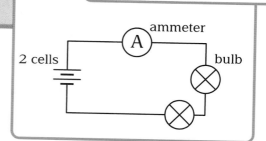

ammeter

2 cells

bulb

Measuring electric current in a series circuit

These three diagrams show the positions in which an ammeter could be connected in this series circuit.

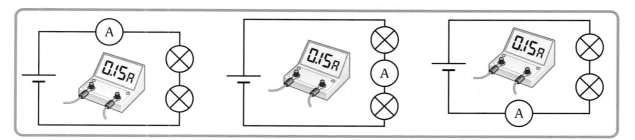

All of these ammeters show the same reading. The electric current is the same all the way around a series circuit. The current does not get used up as it passes through each bulb; it stays the same.

6 What would be the readings on ammeters X and Y in this circuit?

7 How does the current in front of a bulb compare to the current after the bulb?

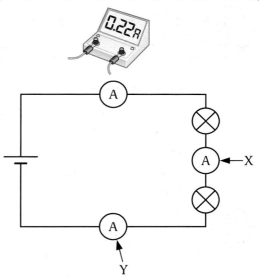

Changing the current

Dimmer switches can be used with household lights to change the brightness of the bulb. The circuits show three different dimmer switch settings and how these affect the brightness of the bulbs.

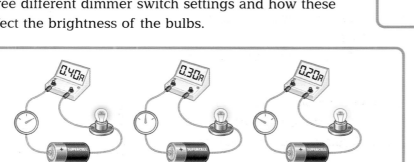

When a current flows in a circuit it has to push its way through each component. It is held back very slightly by each new component it has to push through. This causes **resistance** in a circuit.

As the dimmer switch is turned the bulbs get less bright and the current decreases. A dimmer switch is an example of a **variable resistor**. As you turn the dimmer switch you change the resistance. Increasing the resistance decreases the current and makes the bulb dimmer. Decreasing the resistance increases the current and makes the bulb brighter.

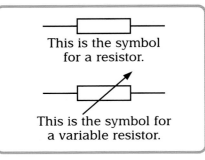

This is the symbol for a resistor.

This is the symbol for a variable resistor.

8 What does a dimmer switch change in a circuit?

9 In a house, when a dimmer switch is turned a bulb gets brighter.

    a Is the resistance increasing or decreasing?

    b Is the current increasing or decreasing?

More bulbs

Bulbs have resistance. They 'resist' or 'slow down' the flow of electric current. Changing the number of bulbs in a series circuit changes the resistance of that circuit. A bulb is one example of a **resistor**. All components cause resistance just like bulbs do.

As bulbs are added to this circuit the total resistance increases and the current decreases. As the current decreases, the bulbs become less bright.

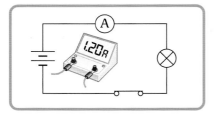 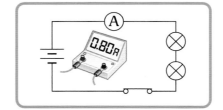 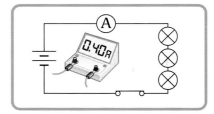

10 Does the total resistance increase or decrease as you add bulbs in a series circuit?

11 When you increase the number of bulbs in a series circuit, what happens to the brightness of those bulbs?

12 Resistors are used in many devices to change the current in that device. Research different uses for resistors and explain what effect the resistor has in each circuit.

7J.3 Energy for the circuit

For an electric current to flow around a circuit there needs to be a source of energy. A cell or battery provides this energy to 'push' the current around the circuit.

Cells and batteries

This picture shows a torch. The energy to make this torch light up is supplied by two **cells**. Two or more cells connected together are called a **battery**.

switch

bulb

battery

Cells and batteries are marked to show their **voltage**. The voltage is measured in **volts**, or 'V' for short.

A higher voltage means that more energy can be supplied. So higher voltage means brighter bulbs.

Be careful! If the voltage is too high the bulb will 'blow' and stop working.

A 1.5V cell.

Two 1.5V cells make a 3.0V battery.

Three 1.5V cells make a 4.5V battery.

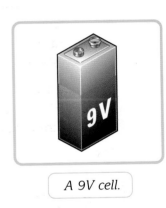

A 9V cell.

1 What is the difference between a cell and a battery?

2 If you connected four 1.5 V cells together, what would be the total voltage?

3 You increase the voltage supplied to a circuit.

   a What would happen to the brightness of the bulbs?

   b Using your answer to part **a**, explain what will happen to the current if the voltage is increased.

Inside a cell

When a cell is connected in a circuit, it pushes the current around the circuit. Inside the cell are chemicals which react together. It is this chemical reaction which pushes the current.

When you connect cells together to make a battery, you need to make sure that the positive end of one cell is connected to the negative end of the next.

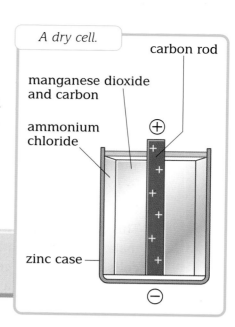

A dry cell.

carbon rod

manganese dioxide and carbon

ammonium chloride

zinc case

4 What chemicals can be found inside a dry cell?

5 Draw a picture of a battery of three cells connected correctly.

Inside a circuit

It can be difficult to picture what happens in an electric circuit because you can't see anything moving. The flow of electric current around a circuit can be compared to the flow of water around a system of pipes.

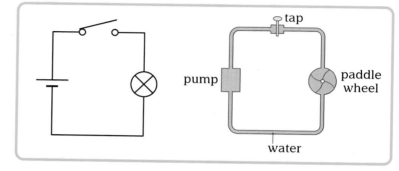

tap

pump

paddle wheel

water

6 **a** What flows around an electric circuit?

b What makes this flow?

7 **a** What would happen to the flow of water if you used two pumps?

b What would be the equivalent in an electric circuit?

Electric circuit		Water circuit	
OBJECT	**JOB**	**OBJECT**	**JOB**
Battery	Pushes the current around the circuit	Pump	Pushes the water around the circuit
Current	Flows around the circuit	Water	Flows around the circuit
Bulb	Uses energy from the current and holds back the current	Paddle wheel	Uses energy from the water and slows the water down
Switch	Breaks the circuit and the flow of current	Tap	Stops the flow of water

8 Some types of cell can be recharged. Find out about the different types of rechargeable cell. Include in your research which chemicals are used in each type of cell. You can also find out how much charge the cell can hold (usually measured in AmpHours).

7J.4 Parallel circuits

So far, the circuits we have studied have been series circuits. The other main type of circuit is called a **parallel** circuit. We will now find out more about parallel circuits and their uses.

Bulbs in parallel

In the series circuits that we have studied so far, there is just one route for the current around the circuit. In parallel circuits there are always junctions where the current can go along two or more different routes.

This circuit shows two bulbs connected in parallel. The electric current leaves the battery. When it gets to junction A some of the current goes through bulb 1 and some through bulb 2. The current splits up. When the current reaches junction B it joins back together again and travels back to the battery. Each part of the circuit, through bulb A and bulb B, is called a 'branch' of the circuit.

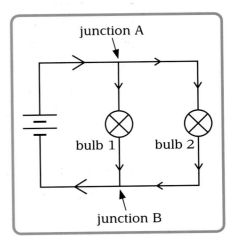

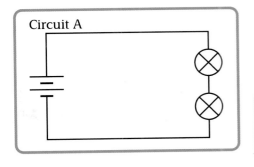

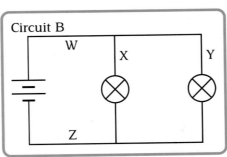

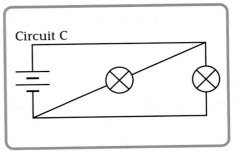

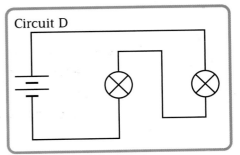

1 Look at the four circuits, A to D.

   a Which circuits are series circuits?

   b Which circuits are parallel circuits?

2 How many routes can the electric current go in:

   a a series circuit?   **b** a parallel circuit?

3 In circuit B the current is at its highest value in the position marked W. Where else would the current be at its highest value: at X, Y or Z?

Electric current in parallel circuits

In a parallel circuit the total current from the battery is the same as the current through each of the separate branches added together. This diagram shows two identical bulbs connected in parallel; these bulbs have the same resistance. The electric current flowing through each bulb is the same, 0.5 A. The current from the battery is the same as the current through the bulbs added together:

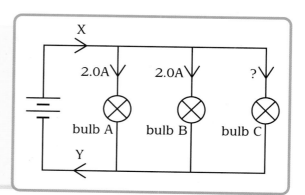

$$0.5\,A + 0.5\,A = 1.0\,A$$

4 In this circuit the three bulbs are identical. Use this circuit diagram to answer the following questions.

a What is the current through bulb C?

b What is the current from the battery?

c What is the current in position X?

d What is the current in position Y?

Bright bulbs in parallel

In a parallel circuit each bulb is connected directly to the battery. The voltage across each bulb is the same as the voltage across the battery. This means that all of the bulbs are bright. You can connect as many bulbs as you like in parallel and they will always stay the same brightness.

When you connect more bulbs in parallel, the current from the battery increases. If you have a lot of bulbs connected the battery will go flat very quickly.

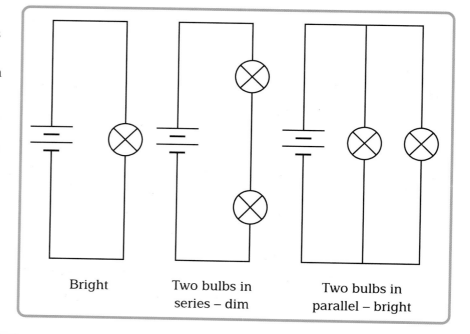

Bright

Two bulbs in series – dim

Two bulbs in parallel – bright

5 If you have four bulbs connected in parallel with a 3 V battery, what will be the voltage across each of the bulbs?

6 As you add lots of bulbs in parallel, what happens to:

a the brightness;   b the total resistance;

c the total current through the bulbs;   d the battery?

Series or parallel

When designing an electrical circuit you need to consider whether a series or a parallel circuit is the best for the intended use. Some Christmas tree lights are wired in series, whereas the lights in houses are wired in parallel.

The parallel circuit is better if you want to control the bulbs separately. This is what you want for the lights in a house. The series circuit can be safer because the current is smaller. A series circuit is useful if you want to light several bulbs which do not need to be very bright.

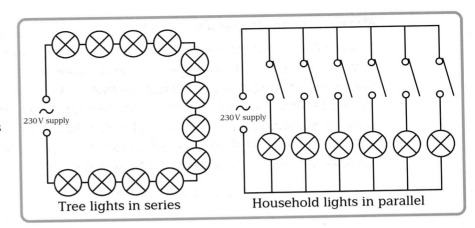

Tree lights in series   Household lights in parallel

Series circuit	Parallel circuit
If one bulb blows they all go out.	If one bulb blows only that one goes out.
One switch operates all of the bulbs.	Each bulb can be turned on and off with its own switch.
The voltage across the power supply is shared between all of the bulbs.	The voltage across each bulb is the same as across the power supply.
The current from the power supply is low.	The current from the power supply is high.

7 What happens to the other bulbs in a series circuit if one bulb blows?

8 Ten bulbs were connected in a series circuit to a power supply. Ten identical bulbs were connected in a parallel circuit to an identical power supply.

   a Which circuit would have the highest voltage across each bulb?

   b In which circuit would the bulbs be brighter?

   c Which circuit do you think would use the most electricity?

9 A Christmas tree light manufacturer wants to design tree lights with 12 bulbs: 3 red, 3 blue, 3 green and 3 yellow. He wants to be able to turn all three bulbs of the same colour on and off together. If a bulb of one colour blows, all of the bulbs of that colour could be off but the other colours should still be capable of being switched on. Design a circuit for this manufacturer.

7J.5 Using electricity safely

Electricity is very useful but also potentially very dangerous. We need to protect ourselves when using electricity, especially when it is **mains electricity**, which uses a higher voltage than batteries.

Safety at home

Most accidents when using electricity in the home are caused by carelessness. If you follow a few sensible safety precautions you will reduce the danger. Here are some reminders of things you must never do.

NEVER use mains appliances in the bathroom

NEVER touch sockets or switches with wet hands

NEVER use appliances with frayed cables or if the cables are repaired with tape

insulating tape

under the tape

wires twisted together

NEVER overload a socket

NEVER pull a plug out by the cable

pull

NEVER leave a kettle lead switched on when disconnected from the kettle

1 List <u>six</u> things you should never do when using mains electricity.

2 How should you pull a plug out of a socket?

3 What could you use as a safe alternative to a mains powered radio in the bathroom?

Fuses

Sometimes a fault in a circuit can cause the electric current to become too big. This can damage electrical appliances. A **fuse** breaks the circuit if the current becomes too big. This stops the appliance from working and therefore protects it. This is the circuit symbol for a fuse:

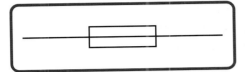

Inside a fuse is a piece of wire, called fuse wire. If the current is too high the fuse wire becomes hot and melts. When the fuse wire melts the circuit is broken and no current can now flow. The word 'fuse' is another word for melt.

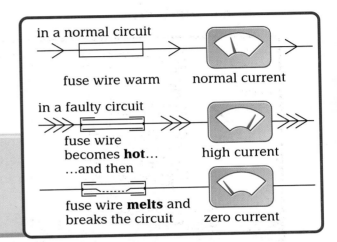

in a normal circuit

fuse wire warm   normal current

in a faulty circuit

fuse wire becomes **hot**... ...and then   high current

fuse wire **melts** and breaks the circuit   zero current

4 a What happens to the wire inside a fuse if the current is too high?

b How does this stop the flow of electric current?

You can find fuses in plugs. The fuse is always connected to the live wire so that no electric current can flow to the appliance if the fuse blows. Fuses have different current ratings; this is the current above which the fuse will blow. The fuse drawn here has a current rating of 5 A. If a current of more than 5 A flows the fuse will blow.

Circuit breakers are often used instead of fuses. These 'cut out' when the current is too high and can be reset by flicking a switch.

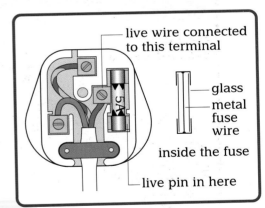

live wire connected to this terminal

glass
metal
fuse wire
inside the fuse

live pin in here

5 A fuse in a plug could be replaced with an iron nail and the appliance would still work. Why must you not do this?

6 Try to find out what values of current rating fuses you can get. For each value list as many appliances as you can which should take this size of fuse.

So far in this unit we have used the idea of electric current and the fact that it flows through circuits. We are now going to consider where the idea of electric current came from and find out a little about the scientists who discovered it.

Luigi Galvani and his frogs

Luigi Galvani was an Italian scientist born in 1737. His main interest was in medicine and how the body works. He worked at the University of Bologna. This is where he started a series of experiments in 1780. As part of his experimental work he was studying the legs of frogs. These frog legs were hung up by copper hooks, on iron railings. Galvani noticed that the frog legs twitched and the muscles contracted.

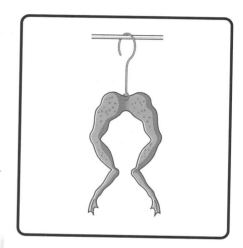

Scientists believed that **nerves** carried messages around the body. Most scientists thought that these nerves were pipes carrying water. Galvani now believed that these nerves carried electrical pulses. This electricity must be generated somewhere inside the body.

1   What is the job of these nerves?
2   What do nerves carry to the muscles?

Alessandro Volta and his cell

Alessandro Volta was another Italian scientist. He was born in 1745. Volta realised that there must be some sort of reaction between the copper hooks, the iron railings and the liquids from inside the frog. It was this reaction which produced the electric current which travelled along the nerves in the frog's legs.

Volta used this information to make the first ever electric cell. He made this cell using discs made of the metals silver and zinc separated by cardboard discs soaked in salt solution. The volt is named after Volta in honour of the fact that he made the first ever electric cell.

3   What did Volta use to make the first electric cell?
4   Which unit is named after Volta?

5   Galvani deduced that electric currents travelled along nerves. Volta made the first battery. How could Volta's battery be used to prove that nerves carry an electric current?

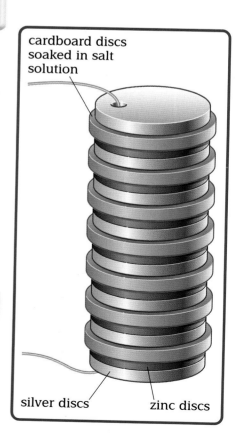

cardboard discs soaked in salt solution

silver discs   zinc discs

You should now understand the key words and key ideas shown below.

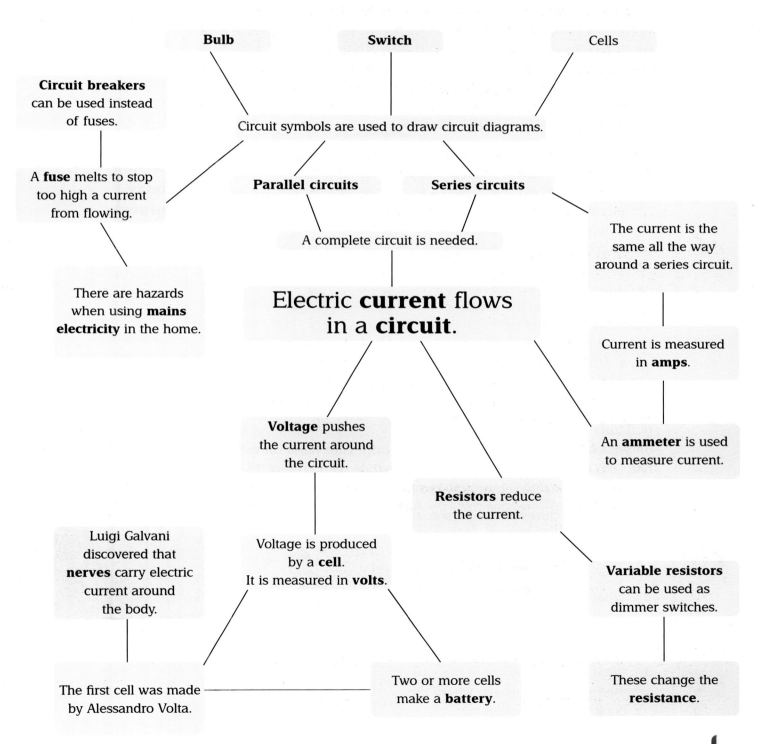

Bulb

Switch

Cells

Circuit breakers can be used instead of fuses.

Circuit symbols are used to draw circuit diagrams.

A **fuse** melts to stop too high a current from flowing.

Parallel circuits

Series circuits

A complete circuit is needed.

The current is the same all the way around a series circuit.

There are hazards when using **mains electricity** in the home.

Electric **current** flows in a **circuit**.

Current is measured in **amps**.

Voltage pushes the current around the circuit.

An **ammeter** is used to measure current.

Resistors reduce the current.

Luigi Galvani discovered that **nerves** carry electric current around the body.

Voltage is produced by a **cell**. It is measured in **volts**.

Variable resistors can be used as dimmer switches.

The first cell was made by Alessandro Volta.

Two or more cells make a **battery**.

These change the **resistance**.

Forces and their effects

In this unit we shall study the effect that different forces have on objects. We shall learn the names of some forces and study ideas connected with the speed of objects.

KEY WORDS
force
newton
stretch
attraction
repulsion
weight
body
gravity
mass
extension
proportional
upthrust
density
volume
friction
lubricant
drag
speed
distance

7K.1 Where we come across forces

In everyday life there are many different examples of **force**. They are all pushes or pulls.

Forces act in pairs

When things touch there are two forces acting in opposite directions, one force on each object. When the legs of a stool touch the floor there are push forces on the legs and push forces on the floor.

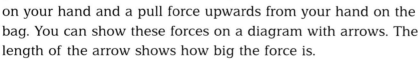

When you carry a bag, the handles and your hand touch each other. Two forces are produced where your hand and the bag touch. There is a pull force downwards from the bag on your hand and a pull force upwards from your hand on the bag. You can show these forces on a diagram with arrows. The length of the arrow shows how big the force is.

Look at the pictures of the person and the book.

1   Does the up or down arrow show the force of the person on the floor?

2   What force is pushing on the bench? What is its direction?

3   What can you say about the size of the forces that happen where the book touches the bench?

Measuring forces

The size of a force is measured in newtons. One **newton** is about the size of pull that you need to lift a small apple. You need a force of about five newtons to pick up a mug of tea. You would need a force of over 1000 newtons to pick up a Sumo wrestler!

You can measure the size of a force with a forcemeter. A forcemeter has a spring inside it. When the force is small the spring does not **stretch** much. When it measures a large force the spring is stretched more. Forcemeters have different ranges so that they can measure different sizes of force.

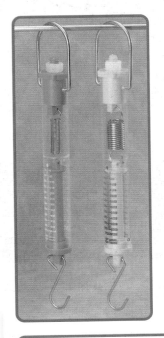

4 **a** What do we use to measure the size of a force?

b What is inside this?

5 Look at the photograph. Which of the two forcemeters do you think will measure the larger force?

Forces between magnets

Two magnets produce a pair of forces whether they are touching or not. If you hold them one way, the magnets will produce a pair of forces that pull the magnets together. This is called **attraction**. If you turn one magnet round they will produce a pair of forces that push the magnets apart. This is called **repulsion**. There is a pair of forces that attract a magnet and a piece of iron or steel. One force acts on the magnet and one acts on the piece of iron or steel to pull them together.

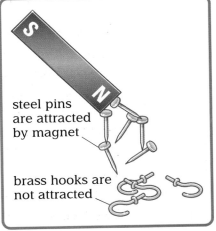

steel pins are attracted by magnet

brass hooks are not attracted

6 Look at the diagram of the fridge. Are the magnet and the fridge door attracting or repelling?

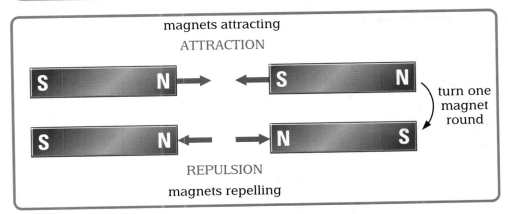

magnets attracting
ATTRACTION

turn one magnet round

REPULSION
magnets repelling

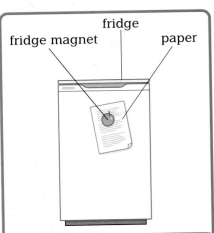

fridge magnet   fridge   paper

The fridge magnet does not attract paper. The fridge magnet and the fridge door attract each other through the paper.

7 Draw a diagram showing the forces that act between the fridge magnet and the fridge. Use arrows to show forces.

7K.2 Weight

Some forces are very important. They have special names. One of these is the force we call weight.

The Earth pulls things towards it

When something is dropped it falls towards the centre of the Earth. This happens because there is a force on it called **weight**. The arrows in this diagram show the direction of this force on objects at different places around the Earth.

Weight is a force that happens whether or not the Earth and the object touch each other. You measure the weight of something when you hang it on a forcemeter.

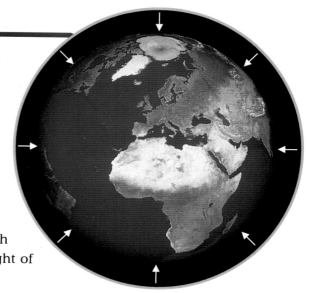

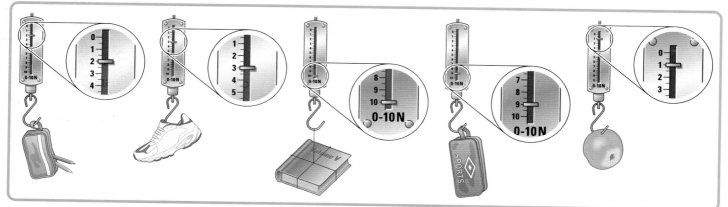

1   Write down the weights of the things shown in the diagram.

2   Which is the heaviest object shown?

3   If the sports bag was full of apples, about how many apples would it have inside it? (Assume the bag alone weighs 1 newton.)

Isaac Newton and gravity

In the 17th century Isaac Newton worked out that every **body** attracted every other body with a force he called **gravity**. (Scientists use the word 'body' when they talk about any object.)

The force of gravity is very weak. You only really notice it when one of the bodies is very heavy like the Earth or the Moon. The force of gravity between the Earth and a golf ball is about half a newton. This is big enough to notice because the Earth has a mass of about six million million million million kilograms. The force of gravity between two golf balls next to each other is so incredibly small it is not noticeable. It is about a two thousand millionth of a newton.

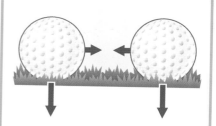

The attraction of gravity between the balls is too small to matter.

The pull of gravity from the Earth keeps the balls on the ground.

The idea of the force of gravity attracting everything is very important even if the force is very small for light objects. Newton used it to explain how all the planets and moons moved in the Solar System, how tides happened, what a comet was and many other things that people did not understand. His idea is still used today to plan space flights.

The pull of gravity from the Earth is what we call weight. The Moon is smaller than the Earth, so the pull of gravity on something on the Moon would be smaller than the pull of gravity on the same thing on the Earth. You weigh less on the Moon!

Distance not to scale

The Earth's gravity is about six times bigger than the Moon's.

4 What is the name for the force that attracts every body to every other body?

5 Why don't you notice the force of gravity acting between two golf balls?

6 When do you notice the force of gravity?

Weight and mass

Mass tells you how much stuff something is made of. Mass is measured in kilograms. Weight is the pull of gravity on the mass. The Earth pulls a 1 kilogram bag of sugar down with a force of about 10 N. If you had the same bag of sugar on the Moon it would still have a mass of 1 kilogram. However, because the gravity on the Moon is a lot less, its weight would be about 1.6 N.

The chart shows the weight of a 100 kg bag of sand in different places in the Universe. Remember that mass doesn't change even though the weight changes.

Location	On Earth	On the Moon	On Jupiter	In deep space	Near to a black hole
Mass	100 kg	100 kg	100 kg	100 kg	100 kg
Weight	1000 N	160 N	5400 N	Almost nothing	Too big to measure. Gravity is so big even light is pulled in. Nothing escapes a black hole!

7 What is the difference between mass and weight?

8 What is the weight of a 3 kg bag of sugar on Earth?

9 Why is the weight of something on the Moon smaller than it is on the Earth?

10 Cookery books give the weights of things in grams and kilograms. What is wrong with that?

7K.3 Stretching materials

When you pull on the end of a spring it gets longer. The size of the **extension** of the spring depends on the size of the force.

Measuring things that stretch

The diagram shows the apparatus you could use and the type of results you get when you do experiments to see how a spring stretches.

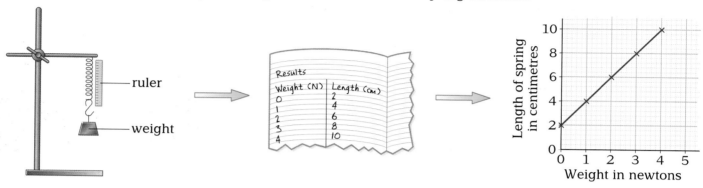

Look at the graph above. The spring is 4 cm long when the pulling force on it is 1 N. When you increase the pulling force by 1 N the spring gets 2 cm longer. This means that the extension goes up by 2 cm every time the pulling force increases by 1 N. If you use twice the size of force you get twice the size of extension. Three times the force gives three times the extension. We say the extension of the spring is **proportional** to the force. The graph is a straight line if this is true.

Sid and Eric perform some experiments for a spring and for a rubber band. Here are the graphs of their results.

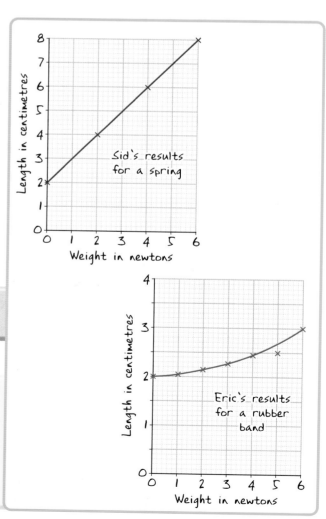

1 What force will make Sid's spring 5 cm long?

2 Do the spring and the rubber band follow the same pattern? Give a reason for your answer.

3 Which of Eric's readings looks like it was recorded wrongly? Give a reason for your answer. What should Eric do about the reading?

Different shape and thickness

Springs made from thicker wire need bigger forces to stretch them than springs made from thinner wire. This effect is used to make springs for forcemeters with different ranges.

Wire also stretches very slightly when you pull it. You have to use a much larger force to stretch a piece of straight wire than the force you need to stretch a spring. Stringed instruments use stretched wires to make musical notes.

The wire is usually called a string even though for many instruments the 'string' is actually a wire made from a metal like steel or from nylon. The string is stretched so it is tight enough to give the right note.

The top E string on an electric guitar needs a force of about 75 N to stretch it into tune. When it is stretched into tune it is about 7 mm longer than when it is slack. The total force on the tailpiece of an electric guitar when it is in tune is about 530 N! That is enough to pick up a 53 kg person.

4   Which type of spring, one made from thick wire or one made from thin wire, needs the bigger force to stretch it?

5   Which substances are the 'strings' on musical instruments usually made from?

6   What type of spring, thick or thin, would you expect to find in a forcemeter with a range of 0 to 0.1 N? Give a reason for your answer.

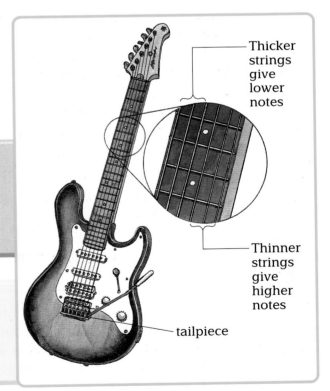

Thicker strings give lower notes

Thinner strings give higher notes

tailpiece

7   Make a list of the places in a home where a spring, wire or elastic substance might be used because it stretches when a force is applied to it.

7K.4 Floating and sinking

Some objects float on water. This happens because a force is felt by an object in water.

Pushing water out of the way

When an object is put into a liquid it has to push some of the liquid out of the way. You can prove this by putting a golf ball into a beaker of water that is full to the brim. The water that is pushed out of the way flows over the rim of the beaker. You can see the effect if you put the same golf ball in a half full beaker with the level of the water marked on. This time the water that is pushed out of the way does not overflow, it moves to make the water level higher on the side of the beaker.

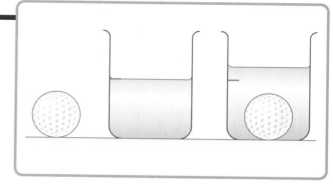

The liquid is pushed out of the way by the golf ball. There is a push up from the liquid on the golf ball. This upwards force is called **upthrust**. The picture shows how you can measure the size of the upthrust for a golf ball.

The upthrust depends on how much liquid is pushed out of the way. You can feel the size of the upthrust using a plastic lunchbox in a sink full of water. When you push it deeper into the water you can feel that the upthrust is bigger because more water is pushed out of the way.

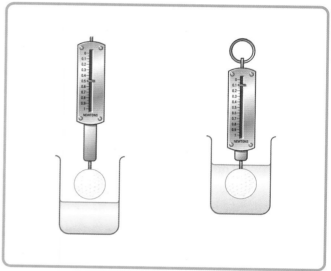

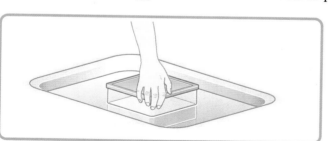

The upthrust is an upwards force from the water. Its effect is to cancel out some of the object's weight. The object seems to weigh less in water than it does in the air.

water ——
upthrust ——
0.5 N
— weight —
2 N   2 N

The block feels like it weighs 1.5 N in water because the upthrust is in the opposite direction to the weight.

1 When an object is put into water:

   a what happens to the height of the water?

   b what is the name for the force produced by the water?

   c what does the size of this force depend on?

Why some things float on water

Some things are light for their size. Lumps of cork, polystyrene ceiling tiles and sticks of balsa wood are examples of things that are light for their size. Blocks of steel, lead and concrete are heavy for their size. If something is light for its size it will float on water. This happens because the upthrust from the water is equal to the weight of the object.

The block of wood shown weighs 1 N. When it is put into water it pushes water out of the way. The upthrust increases as more water is pushed out of the way. When the upthrust is 1 N, the upthrust equals the weight of the wood. The wood floats.

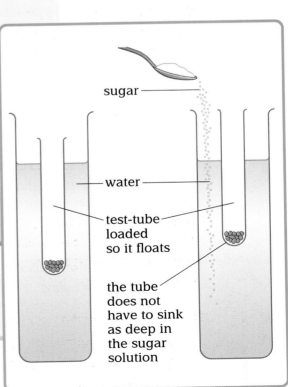

What happens when this mass is added?

Most of the wood needs to be under the water to create an upthrust equal to its weight.

2 What does an object have to do to the water to create an upthrust?

3 How big must the upthrust be for the object to float?

4 What do you think will happen to the block of wood if the 100 g mass is put onto the top of it?
(Hint: A 100 g mass has a weight of 1 N.)

Floating in heavier liquids

If the liquid is heavier than water then you do not need to push as much out of the way to get the same upthrust. You can make a liquid heavier by dissolving something in it. The water in the picture has been made heavier by dissolving sugar in it.

sugar

water

test-tube loaded so it floats

the tube does not have to sink as deep in the sugar solution

5 What has been dissolved in the water to make it heavier?

6 It is easier to float on a calm sea than it is on a calm fresh water lake. Suggest a reason for this.

Comparing densities

You can use a number to describe how heavy something is for its size. This number is called the **density** of the substance. Density is actually a fair way of comparing the mass of different substances. To calculate density you need to know the mass in grams of one centimetre cubed of the substance. This can be calculated using this equation:

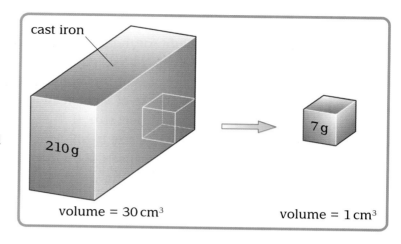

cast iron

210 g

volume = 30 cm³

7 g

volume = 1 cm³

> density = mass ÷ **volume**

For example, the block in the diagram has a mass of 210 grams and a volume of 30 centimetres cubed. Its density is

> 210 grams ÷ 30 centimetres cubed = 7 grams per centimetre cubed.

This means that if you cut 1 centimetre cubed out of it the mass would be 7 grams.

7 How do you work out a density?

8 What does the density tell you?

9 What would the density be for a block of metal with a mass of 350 grams and a volume of 50 centimetres cubed?

The density is a good way of telling if something will float or not.

Solid blocks of substances that float on a liquid have a density lower than the density of the liquid.

10 Look at the pictures. Describe how different materials behave in water and in olive oil.

11 Find out what a Plimsoll line is, who invented it and why.

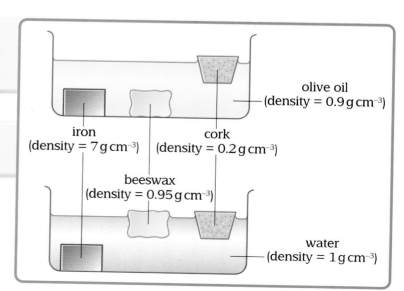

olive oil (density = 0.9 g cm⁻³)

iron (density = 7 g cm⁻³)

cork (density = 0.2 g cm⁻³)

beeswax (density = 0.95 g cm⁻³)

water (density = 1 g cm⁻³)

7K.5 Friction

Friction is the name for a particular type of force. Friction is one of the most important forces in our lives. You couldn't walk without friction. Woven materials like clothes would fall apart without friction!

Places where friction happens

Friction happens when things try to slide past each other. It is a force you get when things touch. Friction forces occur when things are actually sliding and even before they start sliding. Look at the pictures of Eric and Sonja pushing the box.

1   Where does the friction force occur?

2   What is the direction of the friction force compared to the pushing force?

3   What happens to the box when the pushing force is bigger than the friction force?

Reducing friction

Friction is a problem when surfaces need to move over each other. Anything with moving parts has a problem with friction. Friction will wear away a surface where that surface meets another one. Friction also uses up energy. You can show this by rubbing your hands together. The friction soon warms them up! Movement energy is converted to heat energy through friction.

There are three main ways to reduce friction:

- you can make the surfaces smooth;
- you can put a **lubricant** like oil on them;
- you can design the moving parts so they roll on each other rather than slide.

You can judge how much friction there is between an object and a surface by tilting the surface. If the friction force is big, the object will not slide until the surface is quite steep.

Eric and Sonja push the box. It doesn't move.

A friction force balances the pushing force.

The friction force happens where the box touches the floor.

Eric and Sonja push harder. The box still doesn't move.

The friction force gets bigger. It still balances the pushing force.

The friction force is in the opposite direction to the push.

Eric and Sonja push harder still. Now the box moves.

movement

The friction force can't get any bigger. The pushing force is now bigger than the friction force. There is an unbalanced force. So the box moves.

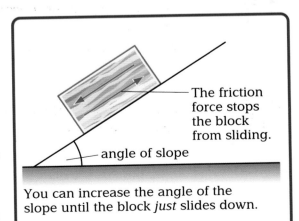

The friction force stops the block from sliding.

angle of slope

You can increase the angle of the slope until the block *just* slides down.

With a tin of beans standing on its flat end, the slope can get to 40° before the tin slides down. If you put the tin on its side, it rolls as soon as there is any slope at all.

about 40°

It takes a steep slope for the tin to slide.

about 3°

The tin rolls much more easily.

Rollers can be used to reduce friction when you are trying to move large blocks of stone. The same idea is used on a small scale in the wheels of a bike. The wheels of a bike turn on sets of ball bearings. These are designed to reduce friction because they roll rather than slide. You can also reduce the friction by using oil on the moving parts. We say that the oil <u>lubricates</u> the moving parts.

4 What does friction do to surfaces?

5 Name a substance that can be used as a lubricant.

6 What <u>three</u> things can you do to reduce the friction between surfaces?

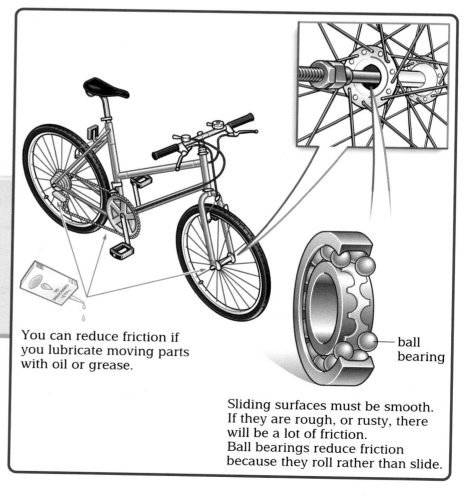

You can reduce friction if you lubricate moving parts with oil or grease.

ball bearing

Sliding surfaces must be smooth. If they are rough, or rusty, there will be a lot of friction.
Ball bearings reduce friction because they roll rather than slide.

Friction can be useful

If there were no friction you could not walk and your shoelaces would be impossible to tie. When you walk you push your foot backwards. The effect of the friction forces between your foot and the floor is to move you forward. This happens because the floor does not move. If you try the same thing off a skateboard, which can move, then you won't get very far because the skateboard moves back instead of you going forward. This happens because the wheels of the skateboard act like rollers and reduce the friction to a very low level.

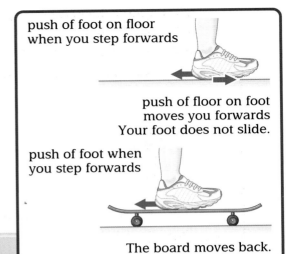

push of foot on floor when you step forwards

push of floor on foot moves you forwards
Your foot does not slide.

push of foot when you step forwards

The board moves back.

7 What is the effect of the friction force between your foot and the floor when you walk?

8 Why is it difficult to step forward off a skateboard?

9 Why is it difficult to walk on ice?

Another friction force

The friction force when something slides through air or a liquid is called **drag**. It slows things down and makes speeding up harder.

People who design racing cars spend a lot of time working out what shape the car has to be to make the drag as low as possible. The same idea is also used to design the shape of cars and vans so they do not use as much petrol. A car with a shape that moves through the air easily does not use as much petrol as a car of the same size going at the same speed with a shape that gives more drag. We say that the shape that goes through the air with less drag is more streamlined.

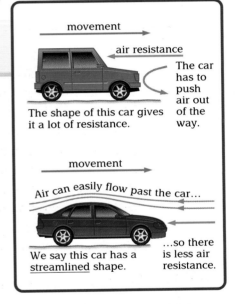

movement

air resistance

The car has to push air out of the way.

The shape of this car gives it a lot of resistance.

movement

Air can easily flow past the car...

...so there is less air resistance.

We say this car has a streamlined shape.

Drag can also be very useful. If you want to slow down the fall of an object you can increase the drag with a parachute. Some plants use the drag of the air to allow their seeds to be dispersed by the wind. The seed can travel a long way on the wind before it hits the ground. This means the new plant growing from the seed will not be competing with the original plant for food and space.

10 What is drag?

11 How can you reduce the drag on something moving through the air?

12 Describe some situations where drag is useful.

7K.6 Moving and stopping

Friction is used to stop things moving. Brakes and tyres are designed to make good use of friction.

Using the brakes

When you want to stop a bike or car you use the brakes. The brakes push on the wheels and produce a friction force. The friction force slows the wheels down. This is an example of where friction is useful.

Even if you have good brakes you need a good grip on the road as well. When you slow down the wheel, you produce a friction force between the road and the wheel that stops you moving forward. If your tyres do not have a good grip the friction force will be too small and you will skid.

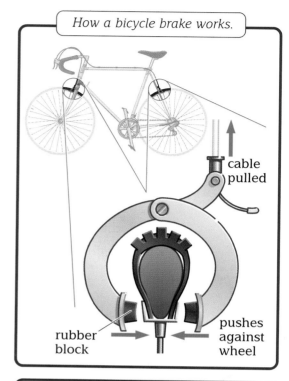
How a bicycle brake works.

cable pulled

rubber block

pushes against wheel

This tyre is old and very worn.

This tyre is brand new.

Did you know that a bald tyre actually grips a dry road better than a new tyre? But there is a problem when the road is slightly damp or wet. On wet or damp roads the bald tyre will slip all over the place and cause accidents. There is a law against driving around with bald tyres.

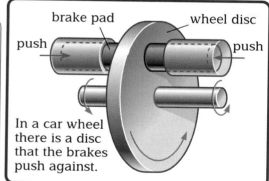
brake pad

wheel disc

push

push

In a car wheel there is a disc that the brakes push against.

1 What pushes on a wheel to slow down a bike or car?
2 When the wheel slows down what type of force is produced between the wheel and the road?

3 What might happen to a car that is slowing down if the friction force on the tyres is too small?

Speed and stopping

When you ride a bike or travel in a car you describe how fast you travel by the speed. **Speed** tells you how far you go in a certain time. A speed of 30 miles per hour (mph) means you would travel 30 miles in one hour if you kept

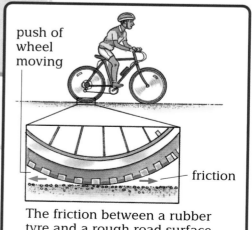
push of wheel moving

friction

The friction between a rubber tyre and a rough road surface moves the bike forwards.

going at that speed. A speed of 20 km/h means you would travel 20 kilometres in one hour if you kept going at that speed. The maximum speed that traffic is allowed to go at in built-up areas is 30 mph, which is about 48 km/h.

The speed of a car affects how long it takes to stop. The faster you are going, the longer it takes to stop.

The blue stripe shows the **distance** you travel while you are just thinking about stopping. If a driver is tired, affected by medicines, under the influence of alcohol or drugs, or even just distracted by a conversation with a passenger, the thinking distance can be a lot longer because reactions are slower.

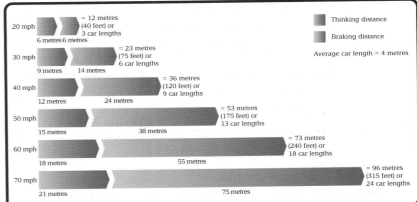

The red stripe shows the distance you travel once you start to brake. If the road is slippery or the tyres are worn or if you start to skid then the braking distance will be a lot further.

This chart is taken from the Highway Code.

4   What is the total stopping distance at 30 mph?

5   Why is the speed limit only 30 mph in built-up areas?

6   What type of things can make the total stopping distance for a car longer than those shown in the chart?

Showing a bike ride on a graph

If you plot a graph of the distance travelled against the time you take you get something called a distance/time graph. This type of graph gives you a picture of what is happening on the journey. A horizontal part of the line means you have stopped. A steep part of the line represents a high speed.

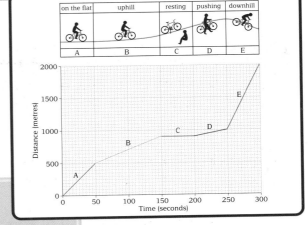

7   On which part of the journey is the speed of the cyclist the highest?

8   On which part of the journey is the speed of the cyclist zero?

9   Sketch a distance/time graph to show your journey to school.

You should now understand the key words and key ideas shown below.

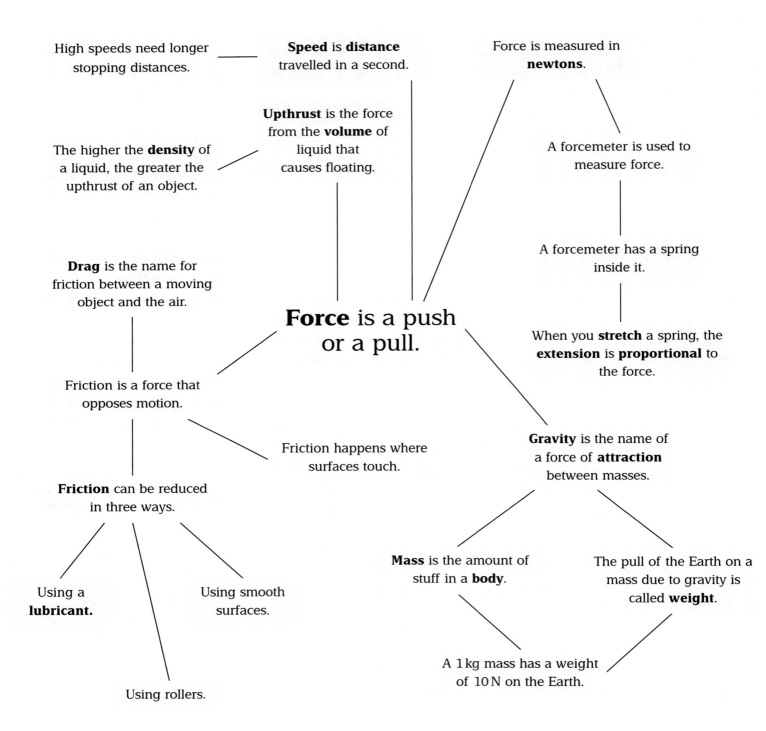

High speeds need longer stopping distances.

Speed is **distance** travelled in a second.

Force is measured in **newtons**.

Upthrust is the force from the **volume** of liquid that causes floating.

The higher the **density** of a liquid, the greater the upthrust of an object.

A forcemeter is used to measure force.

Drag is the name for friction between a moving object and the air.

A forcemeter has a spring inside it.

Force is a push or a pull.

When you **stretch** a spring, the **extension** is **proportional** to the force.

Friction is a force that opposes motion.

Friction happens where surfaces touch.

Gravity is the name of a force of **attraction** between masses.

Friction can be reduced in three ways.

Using a **lubricant.**

Using smooth surfaces.

Mass is the amount of stuff in a **body**.

The pull of the Earth on a mass due to gravity is called **weight**.

A 1 kg mass has a weight of 10 N on the Earth.

Using rollers.

The Solar System and beyond

In this unit we shall be studying the Earth and our neighbours in space, such as the Sun, the Moon and the planets. We will also consider our place in the wider Universe.

astronomer
axis
orbit
seasons
hemisphere
arc
body
star
solar
planet
satellite
lunar
phase
eclipse
Solar System
asteroid belt
galaxy
Universe
constellation

7L.1 The Earth in space

For thousands of years, people have wondered what causes day and night and the changing seasons. They have watched the Sun, Moon and stars move across the sky and they wondered if the Earth is moving too. Scientists who study these things are called **astronomers**.

Days like these

At dawn, we see the Sun rise in the East. It moves across the sky during the day and sets in the West. For many centuries most people thought this was because the Sun travels around the Earth.

Some people disagreed. In the sixteenth century a Polish monk called Nicolaus Copernicus realised that if the Sun stayed still and the Earth spun, we would see the same effect.

We say that the Earth spins on its **axis**. Imagine you had a giant cocktail stick and could push it right through the centre of the Earth from the North Pole, to the South Pole. This would show the line of the Earth's axis. It takes 24 hours for the Earth to make one complete turn on its axis. We call this a day.

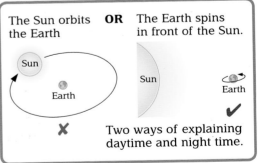

The Sun orbits the Earth **OR** The Earth spins in front of the Sun.

Two ways of explaining daytime and night time.

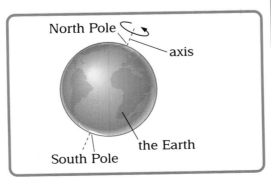

North Pole

axis

the Earth

South Pole

Unit 7L   45

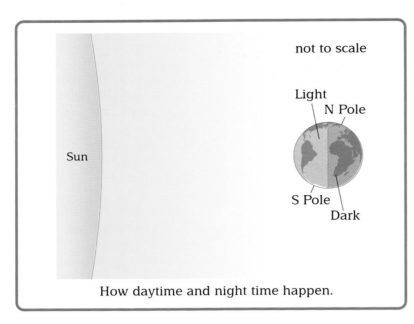

not to scale

Light
N Pole
Sun
S Pole
Dark

How daytime and night time happen.

Each star appears to move around the Pole Star.

Like the Sun and Moon, the stars seem to move across the sky. Only the Pole Star stays in the same place. This gives us further evidence that the Earth is spinning.

Only the parts of the Earth's surface facing the Sun are lit. On those parts it is daytime. The parts of the Earth's surface that are facing away from the Sun are in darkness; it is night time there.

The Earth never stands still. There are always parts of the Earth's surface that are moving into the light and other parts moving out of the light.

In the first picture the UK is facing the Sun and so it is daytime there. Australia is facing away from the Sun and it is night time there. India is just entering the dark side, so it is dusk.

12 hours later it is night time in the UK and daytime in Australia. In India it is getting light, so it is dawn.

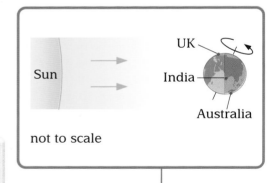

Sun

UK
India
Australia

not to scale

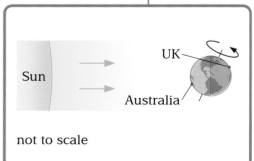

Sun

UK
Australia

not to scale

1 In which direction do we look to see the Sun rise?

2 How long does it take for the Earth to spin once on its axis?

3 If it is midday in the UK, what time do you think it might be in:

a India; b central Australia; c America's East coast?

4 What are time zones? Find out how they are used.

Why we have years

We know that the Earth spins. At the same time, the Earth travels around the Sun. We say that it **orbits** the Sun. We call the time it takes for the Earth to orbit the Sun a year.

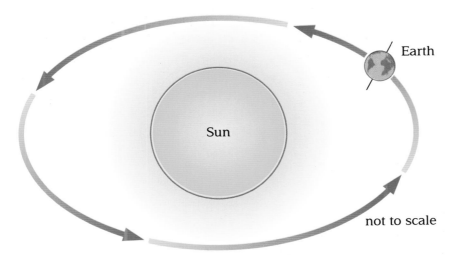

Earth

Sun

not to scale

The Earth takes a year to orbit the Sun.

During a year, the Earth makes $365\frac{1}{4}$ turns on its axis. So a year is really $365\frac{1}{4}$ days long! We can't have a $\frac{1}{4}$ day on our calendars so we round down to 365 days most years. Every fourth year, we catch up by adding a whole day. We call this a <u>leap year</u>.

5 How long is a year on Earth?

6 Explain why an Earth year is this length.

7 Why do we have leap years?

8 The orbit of the Earth around the Sun is not a perfect circle. It is a shape called an <u>ellipse</u>. Find out what an ellipse is and draw an elliptical orbit.

7L.2 The four seasons

As we go through a year, we notice the temperature changing. The number of hours of daylight in a day also changes. We can describe these changes by dividing the year into four **seasons**: spring, summer, autumn and winter.

We have seasons because the Earth's axis is tilted. This means that different parts of the Earth are tilted towards the Sun or away from it during the year.

We call the top half of the Earth the <u>northern hemisphere</u> and the bottom half the <u>southern hemisphere</u>. When your hemisphere is tilted towards the Sun, you are in summer. When your **hemisphere** is tilted away from the Sun, you are in winter.

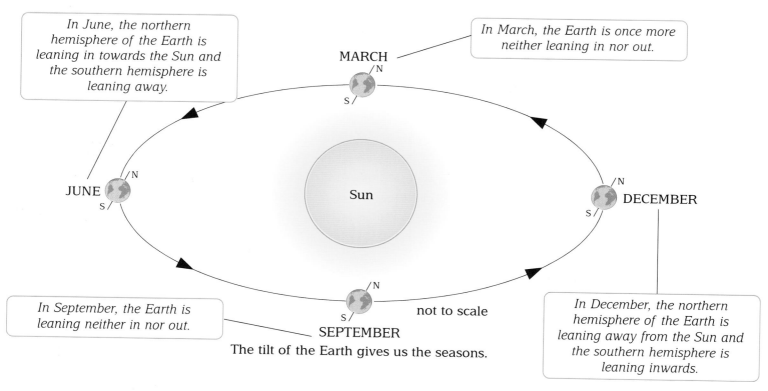

In June, the northern hemisphere of the Earth is leaning in towards the Sun and the southern hemisphere is leaning away.

In March, the Earth is once more neither leaning in nor out.

MARCH

JUNE

Sun

DECEMBER

not to scale

In September, the Earth is leaning neither in nor out.

SEPTEMBER

The tilt of the Earth gives us the seasons.

In December, the northern hemisphere of the Earth is leaning away from the Sun and the southern hemisphere is leaning inwards.

1 When it is summer in the UK, what season is it in Australia?

2 Name <u>five</u> countries in which it is summer at the same time as in the UK.

3 Find out where the Equator is. What do you think the seasons will be like there?

Why it is warmer in summer

One of the main differences between summer and winter is temperature. The tilt of the Earth's axis and the curve of the Earth's surface are the causes of this.

In summer, the rays of light from the Sun shine on a smaller surface area than they do in winter. This means that the rays are more concentrated and they have more effect. The part of the Earth that is tilted towards the Sun becomes warmer.

In winter, the Sun's rays are shining on a larger surface area than they do in summer. The Sun's rays are less concentrated, so the Earth's surface does not get so warm.

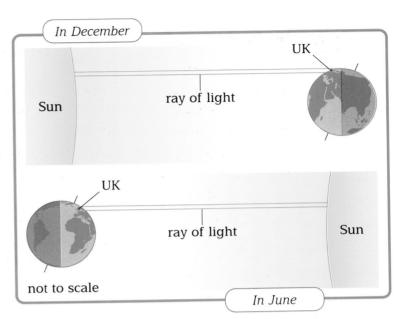

In December

Sun

ray of light

UK

UK

ray of light

Sun

not to scale

In June

 4 Why is it warmer in summer than in winter?

5 Why can't the UK and New Zealand have summer at the same time?

There is a second reason for summer being warmer than winter. In summer daytime lasts longer. This means that the Sun's rays have longer to heat the surface. This helps to raise the temperature.

Why we have more hours of daylight in summer

The second main difference between winter and summer is the length of daylight in a day. It takes 24 hours for the Earth to turn once on its axis, but night time and daytime are hardly ever equal.

The Earth's axis is at an angle to the line that divides daylight from night. In June the northern hemisphere spends more time in daylight than in darkness as it spins. It is summer there.

In December, the northern hemisphere spends less time in daylight than in darkness as it spins. It is winter there.

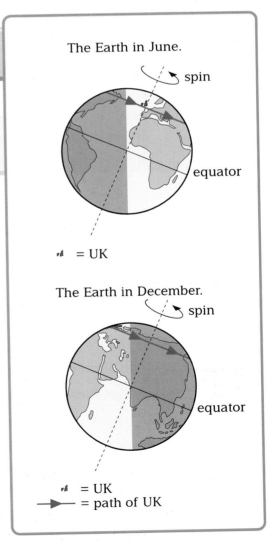

The Earth in June.

spin

equator

⚓ = UK

The Earth in December.

spin

equator

⚓ = UK

→ = path of UK

The part of the Earth which is in summer is tilted towards the Sun, so the Sun appears to be higher in the sky.

When the hours of daylight are long in summer, the Sun rises further back than East, towards Northeast. It then moves high into the sky, passing right overhead. It sets further round than West, towards Northwest. When the hours of daylight are short in winter, the Sun rises less far back, towards Southeast. It moves only a short distance up into the sky and sets only a little way round, towards Southwest. The shape of the Sun's path through the sky is called an **arc**.

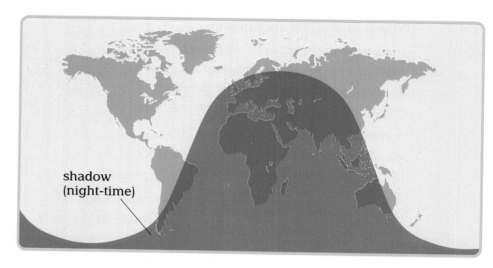

shadow
(night-time)

6   Is the Sun's arc through the sky bigger in summer or winter?

7   In which month does the northern hemisphere have most hours of daylight?

8   In which month does the northern hemisphere have fewest hours of daylight?

9   In summer, how does the length of daylight on the Equator compare with the length of daylight in the UK?

7L.3 Lights in space

When you look up at the sky on a clear night away from street lights, you can see lots of dots of light.

- Some of these are stars.

- Some of these are planets.

- Some may even be manmade satellites in space.

Scientists who study this subject call the different objects in space **bodies**. We are going to explore how we see these bodies and consider the difference between them.

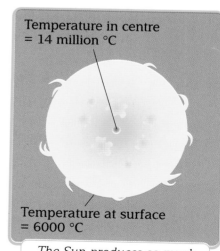

Temperature in centre
= 14 million °C

Temperature at surface
= 6000 °C

The Sun produces so much light that looking at it is dangerous. It is so bright it can damage the sensitive parts of your eye.

Stars

A **star** is a body that gives out its own light. We call this a <u>luminous</u> body. The nearest star to the Earth is the Sun. It looks bigger than all the other stars because it is much closer to the Earth than the others. Stars are like giant nuclear bombs that are exploding all the time. Things to do with the Sun are said to be **solar**.

Planets

Some stars have **planets** in orbit around them. There are nine planets orbiting the Sun. The Earth is one of them. Planets are giant lumps of rock or balls of gas. They do not give out their own light in the same way as stars do. We can only see these planets because they reflect the Sun's light. A planet is a <u>non-luminous</u> body.

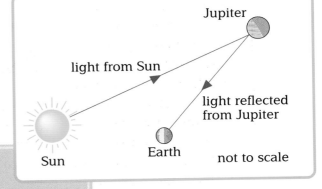

1   Why does the Sun look so much bigger than other stars?

2   Which types of body in space give out their own light?

3   Which types of body do not give out their own light but reflect it?

The Moon

The Moon is the closest body in space to the Earth. It orbits the Earth, so it is called a **satellite** of the Earth. Like the planets, the Moon does not give out its own light; it reflects light from the Sun. Things to do with the Moon are said to be **lunar**.

Phases of the Moon

Just as with the Earth, half of the Moon is in sunlight and half is in darkness. We can only see the part of the Moon that is facing us and is reflecting the sunlight. The amount we can see varies, day by day.

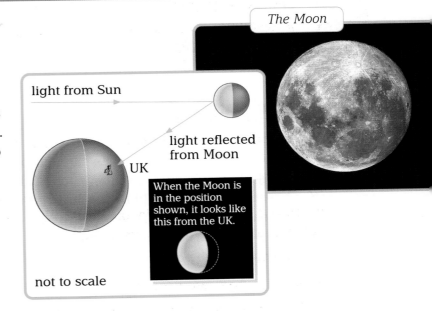

The Moon

The Moon takes 28 days to orbit the Earth. We call this a <u>lunar month</u>. The lunar month starts when we can see just a thin crescent of the Moon. We call this a New Moon.

As the Moon moves around the Earth, it shows us more of the side lit by the Sun. The crescent gets larger. We say it waxes.

When the light side of the Moon is completely facing us, we call it a Full Moon. It looks like a disc. If there are no clouds, a Full Moon can reflect enough light to see by.

The Moon continues to move and gradually less sunlight is reflected to us. The Moon becomes a crescent again as it wanes. At the end of the lunar month the side of the Moon that is in shadow is facing us. Light is not being reflected towards the Earth, and the Moon seems to disappear.

These stages that we see are known as the **phases** of the Moon.

4   What are the names given to bodies that orbit:

    a a star?   **b** a planet?

5   How long does it take for the Moon to orbit the Earth?

6   If the Moon were a luminous body would we see it wax and wane?

7   Imagine you lived on the Moon. Would the Earth always look the same to you? Explain your answer.

7L.4 The Sun and the Moon

If we look at the Sun and the Moon from Earth, they appear to be about the same size. But this is just an illusion. The Sun is actually 400 times bigger than the Moon. If the Sun was the size of a house, the Moon would be the size of a mouse. However, the Sun is nearly 400 times further away from the Earth than the Moon is. The difference in their sizes is cancelled out by the difference in their distances from the Earth.

1   Is the Sun or the Moon bigger?

2   Is the Sun or the Moon closer to the Earth?

WARNING: Never look directly at the Sun (even with sunglasses on). You could damage your eyesight.

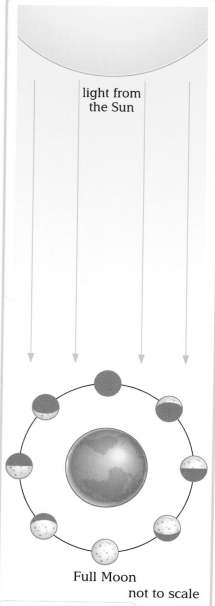

light from the Sun

Full Moon

not to scale

Phases of the Moon.

the setting Sun

the Moon in exactly the same direction at a different time

The Sun and the Moon look the same size.

Solar eclipse

A solar **eclipse** occurs when the Moon passes between the Sun and the Earth so that the three bodies line up. The Moon casts a shadow on the surface of the Earth. The part of the Earth where the shadow falls will become dark, even though it is really daytime there!

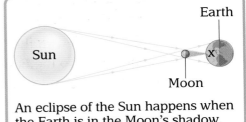

An eclipse of the Sun happens when the Earth is in the Moon's shadow.

x = total eclipse   not to scale

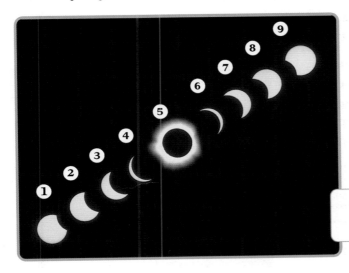

Nine photos of the stages of a total solar eclipse. Number 5 shows totality.

There was a total solar eclipse in August 1999. Across a large section of the world different countries came into the shadow of the Moon, and people were suddenly in complete darkness for just a few minutes. People near the edge of the shadow saw a partial eclipse. This is when the Moon doesn't block out the Sun completely.

3   What causes a solar eclipse?

4   What is the difference between a total eclipse and a partial eclipse?

You might think there should be an eclipse every lunar month. This is not what happens! The orbit of the Moon around the Earth is at a slight angle compared to the orbit of the Earth around the Sun. This means that the Earth, Moon and Sun do not line up very often.

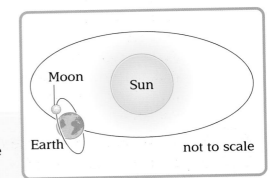

not to scale

5   When there is a total solar eclipse, the part of the Earth in the Moon's shadow becomes dark. Find out what else happens because of this sudden darkness.

Lunar eclipse

A lunar eclipse occurs when the Sun, Earth and Moon line up with the <u>Earth</u> in the middle. The Moon falls into the Earth's shadow. You would expect the Moon to completely disappear because there would be no light reaching it, but this is not quite what happens. The Earth's atmosphere bends some light from the Sun around to the Moon. This means that the Moon appears to be a red or orange colour. Again, because the Moon's orbit is at an angle to the Earth's orbit, lunar eclipses are much rarer than you might expect.

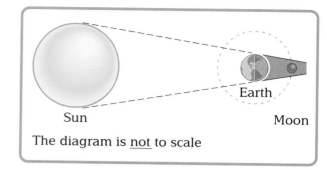

The diagram is <u>not</u> to scale

6 What causes a lunar eclipse?

7 Why does the Moon not disappear completely?

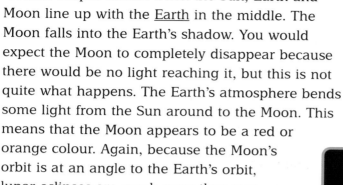

Nine photos of a lunar eclipse.

7L.5 The Solar System

Astronomers have discovered that there are nine planets orbiting the Sun. The Earth is one of them. We call this collection of Sun and planets the **Solar System**.

It took several centuries for astronomers to find all these planets. This was because we can't see some of them without telescopes. Early telescopes were not powerful enough to show us the most distant bodies in the Solar System.

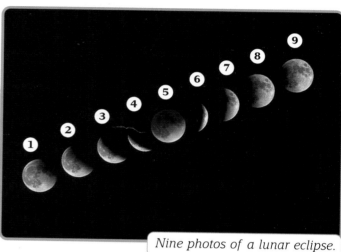

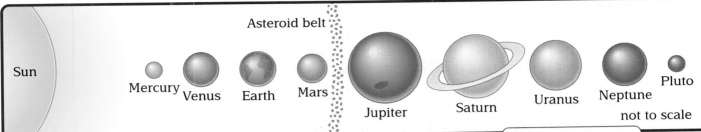

Asteroid belt

Sun

Mercury Venus Earth Mars Jupiter Saturn Uranus Neptune Pluto

not to scale

The Solar System.

Sometimes it is easier to remember a list if you can think of a saying with words that start with the same letters as the items in the list. This kind of saying is called a 'mnemonic'.

My	**V**ery	**E**asy	**M**ethod	**J**ust	**S**peeds	**U**p	**N**aming	**P**lanets
Mercury	**V**enus	**E**arth	**M**ars	**J**upiter	**S**aturn	**U**ranus	**N**eptune	**P**luto

Astronomers find out a lot about the planets by studying their journeys round the Sun. We say they study the planets' motion.

Planet	Distance from Sun (million km)	Diameter of planet (km)	Time taken for one orbit (Earth years)	Time taken for one spin (Earth days)
Mercury	58	4800	0.25	59
Venus	107	12 200	0.65	243
Earth	149	12 800	1.0	1
Mars	228	6800	1.9	1
Jupiter	778	142 600	12	10 hours
Saturn	1427	120 200	29	10 hours
Uranus	2870	49 000	84	11 hours
Neptune	4497	50 000	165	16 hours
Pluto	5900	2287	248	6.5

Mercury, Venus, Earth and Mars are sometimes called the <u>rocky planets</u> because they have a surface that is made from rock. Jupiter, Saturn, Uranus and Neptune are large balls of gas and are called the <u>gas giants</u>. Astronomers are not sure whether Pluto is made from rock or from ice. There is also an **asteroid belt** orbiting the Sun between Mars and Jupiter. Asteroids are lumps of rock that are not big enough to count as planets. They might have come from a planet that broke up a long time ago.

1 Which planet is closest to the Sun?

2 Which is the biggest planet?

3 Which planet's day is the same length as Earth's day?

4 Which planet has the longest year?

Travel to the planets

Science fiction books and films often involve Martians (people from Mars) landing on the Earth. It's more likely that Earthlings will land on Mars. Small unmanned spaceships full of scientific equipment have already landed on the surface of Venus and Mars. We call these machines probes. A few people have walked on the Moon.

5 Why do you think we know more about Venus and Mars than the other planets?

The surface of Mars.

6 Pluto has a moon. Unlike the Earth's moon, Pluto's moon is nearly as big Pluto itself. Some astronomers think of this moon as our Solar System's tenth planet. Try to find out as much about the moon of Pluto as you can – including its name!

7L.6 Beyond the Solar System

Just as the Earth is one planet amongst nine in the Solar System, so the Sun is one star amongst millions. When we look into the night sky we can see some of them.

Where do stars go during daytime?

The Sun is so much closer to us than any other star that its light appears much brighter. It is so bright that we cannot see the light coming from the other stars. This doesn't mean that they are not there during the day. It is just that we cannot see them.

The Milky Way

A **galaxy** is a group of millions of stars. The Milky Way is our local galaxy. The whole Solar System orbits the centre of the Milky Way and it takes millions of years to complete one orbit. If you look into the night sky and see a band of stars across the middle of the sky, you are looking into the Milky Way.

This illustration shows a spiral galaxy. The Milky Way is a spiral galaxy. The Sun is about two thirds of the way out from the centre. It takes light about 100 000 years to cross the Milky Way.

1 Why does the Sun appear to be so much brighter than the other stars?

2 What is the name of the galaxy that includes our Solar System?

3 Draw a sketch of our galaxy and show where our Solar System is.

The Universe

Just as the Sun is one of millions of stars in the Milky Way, the Milky Way is one of millions of galaxies that make up the **Universe**.

It is very difficult to imagine how big the Universe must be. The furthest any person has been from the Earth is to the Moon. That is 400 000 km away, but this is a very small distance compared with the distance to the edge of the Solar System. The next nearest star is 40 000 000 000 000 km away. Even this is a very small distance compared with the distance to the edge of just our galaxy.

Galaxies are spread out thinly with big spaces between them and they are moving away from each other at great speed.

There are millions of galaxies and millions of stars in each galaxy. Even if only some of these stars have planets orbiting them, there will still be billions of planets in the Universe. For life to exist on any of these planets the conditions need to be just right. Living things need an atmosphere to breathe, water and a suitable temperature. Could someone be watching you from another planet as you read this?

Constellations

Stars seem to make shapes and patterns in the sky. We call these patterns **constellations**. Some people believe that the stars control our personality and our fate. You may recognise names like Leo the Lion and the Plough.

If you follow the line of the two right-hand stars in the Plough you can find the Pole Star. The Pole Star shows you which way is North. People have used it for centuries to help them find their way.

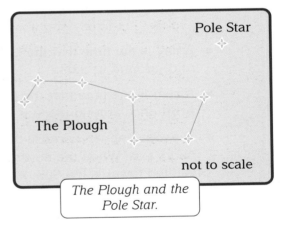

The Plough and the Pole Star.

4   How do the galaxies move in relation to each other?

5   Why is it useful to be able to find the Pole Star?

6   Why might sailors who navigated by the stars have difficulty if they sailed from the UK to Australia?

7   Name as many constellations as you can.

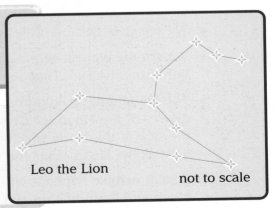

You should now understand the key words and key ideas shown below.

Key words

axis
season
eclipse
hemisphere
lunar
satellite

arc
astronomer
Universe
star
galaxy
Solar System

constellation
orbit
planet
asteroid belt
body
solar

Key ideas

- A day is the time that the Earth takes to spin once around its **axis**.

- A year is the time that the Earth takes to **orbit** once around the Sun.

- **Seasons** happen because the Earth is tilted on its axis. When the northern hemisphere is tilted towards the Sun, it is summer there.

- The days are longer in summer because the Sun's **arc** is bigger. This happens because of the tilt of the Earth's axis.

- We see stars because they are luminous.

- We see the planets because they reflect the light from the Sun. They are non-luminous.

- The Moon reflects light from the Sun; the phases of the Moon are caused by only seeing the side of the Moon which is in the Sun's light as the Moon orbits the Earth.

- A solar **eclipse** happens when the Sun, Moon and Earth line up and the Moon is in the middle.

- A lunar eclipse happens when the Sun, Moon and Earth line up and the Earth is in the middle.

- Nine **planets** have been found in the **Solar System**: Mercury, Venus, Earth, Mars, Jupiter, Saturn, Uranus, Neptune and Pluto.

- The nine planets orbit the Sun and these orbits take different times to complete.

- The Solar System is in a **galaxy** called the Milky Way.

- The Milky Way is one of many galaxies that make up the **Universe**.

- The Earth is the only planet that we know of that can support life.

- The stars appear to move across the night sky because the Earth is rotating.

Heating and cooling

In this unit we shall study heating and cooling and learn how substances behave when they heat up and cool down. We also learn about thermometers and how heat energy is transferred from one place to another.

KEY WORDS

temperature
thermometer
Celsius
degrees
heat energy
joule
conduction
thermal insulators
convection
radiation
melting point
evaporation
boiling point
condensation

8I.1 Measuring how hot things are

PROFESSOR ASSAM IS FLYING IN TO LONDON FROM INDIA.

HIS OLD FRIEND DOCTOR CHILBLAIN, AN EXPERT IN LOW TEMPERATURE PHYSICS, LEAVES HIS LAB IN ICELAND ABOUT THE SAME TIME.

THEY ARE BOTH MET AT HEATHROW BY HIS COUSIN INDIRA WHO LIVES IN LONDON.

PROFESSOR ASSAM FEELS COLD. DOCTOR CHILBLAIN FEELS TOO HOT. INDIRA THINKS THEY ARE BOTH WRONG. AFTER ALL IT IS JUNE AND VERY PLEASANT WEATHER IN LONDON.

People judge how hot or cold things are by the feelings they get from their skin. There is a problem with this. Your estimate depends on where your skin has just been! If you move from a hot place to a cool place you will think it is colder than it actually is. How hot or cold something is is called **temperature**. To get an accurate temperature you need something that always gives the same answer no matter where it has just been. Your skin is no good for this! We use an instrument called a **thermometer**.

There are many different types of thermometers. Some work by electricity, some use a substance that changes colour, others use a liquid that expands and contracts when the temperature changes. The differences do not matter because they all give a reliable measurement of the temperature.

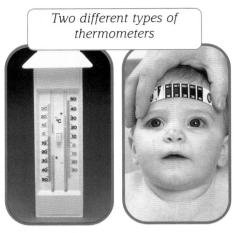
Two different types of thermometers

1   What is the name of the instrument used to measure temperature?
2   What does the temperature of something tell us?

3   Explain why using your skin to estimate temperature can be unreliable.

The Celsius scale

Over the years, many temperature scales have been used. One of the first scientists to try measuring temperature was Galileo. He invented the first thermometer in 1600. It was not very good by today's standards but it was a start. It was based on the expansion of air.

Over the next 150 years several different scientists worked on improving Galileo's ideas. In 1742, Anders Celsius, a Swedish scientist, invented a simple temperature scale with 100 divisions. The 0 mark and the 100 mark could be found by using melting ice and boiling water, so it was easy for anyone to make a thermometer.

This scale is called the **Celsius** scale in honour of Anders Celsius. A temperature of twenty **degrees** Celsius is written as 20 °C.

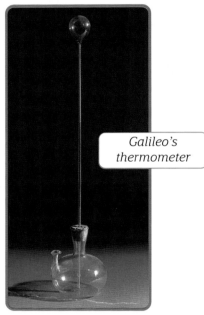
Galileo's thermometer

4   What is the name of the scale used for measuring temperature in everyday work in science?
5   How should you write a temperature of 30 degrees Celsius?

6   What is the temperature range in Britain, from a cold winter's day to a hot summer's day?

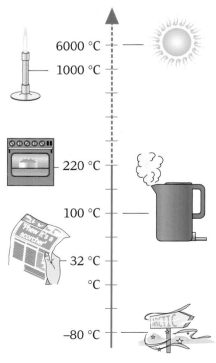

6000 °C
1000 °C
220 °C
100 °C
32 °C
°C
−80 °C

8I.2 Changing the temperature

Heat energy and temperature are different things. This section looks at the differences between them.

Temperature tells us how hot something is. A boiling kettle contains water at a temperature of 100 °C. We say the temperature of the water goes up because it has been provided with **heat energy**. Even though the water in a swimming pool is at a lower temperature than the water in a kettle, the swimming pool contains much more heat energy because it contains much more water. Like all types of energy, heat energy is measured in units called **joules**. The symbol for the joule is J, so 100 joules is written as 100 J.

1 What do you supply to something to make its temperature go up?

2 Find out who James Prescott Joule was and why the unit for energy was named after him.

From high to low

Heat energy moves from high temperature areas to low temperature areas. Something at a high temperature can transfer heat energy to something that is cold. The temperature of the cold object will rise. The temperature of the hot object will fall unless it has a supply of energy to keep its temperature up. For example, if a house is heated so that the temperature inside is higher than outside, heat energy will move out through the walls and windows. Also, if you open a fridge, heat energy moves from the room into the fridge because the room is at a higher temperature. We <u>never</u> say that 'cold moves'.

3 What can move from a hot object to a cold object?

4 What will happen to the temperature of a cold object if it is supplied with heat energy from a hot object?

5 If you put a piece of hot metal into a cold drink, the drink will warm up. Explain why this happens and what happens to the metal.

8I.3 Hot to cold

Heat energy spreads out from hot places to cold places. It does this in a special way in solids.

Conducting the heat energy

Imagine a block of solid material with one end hot and the other end cold.

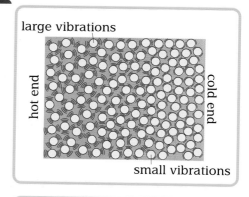

large vibrations

hot end

cold end

small vibrations

The left-hand side is heated with a Bunsen burner. The particles on the left vibrate quickly because that end of the block has a high temperature. Because the particles in a solid are close together, movement gets passed along to the particles on the right. The temperature on the right will start to rise as heat passes energy along the bar.

We say that heat energy has been transferred along the bar. This is called **conduction**. It is the only way heat travels through solids.

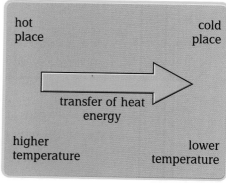

hot place

cold place

transfer of heat energy

higher temperature

lower temperature

1   When heat passes along a solid, what is passed from particle to particle inside the solid?

2   What is the name for the process that takes place when heat travels along a solid, passing from particle to particle?

Some solids conduct heat energy better than others

Sally and Harry have just made some tea. Harry has poured his into a metal mug. Sally has chosen a ceramic mug. Harry learns about conduction the hard way!

Metals are good conductors of heat. The particle vibrations move through metals easily. Other substances like wood, plastic, clay and cloth are poor conductors of heat. We call them heat insulators. They are also called **thermal insulators**.

Even though all metals conduct heat well, some metals are better at it than others. Copper is one of the best. Really expensive cooking pans often have copper in the base to help the transfer of heat energy from the flame to the food.

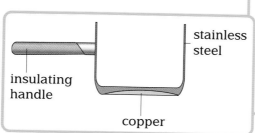

insulating handle

stainless steel

copper

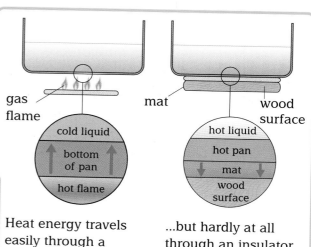

gas flame

mat

wood surface

cold liquid

bottom of pan

hot flame

hot liquid

hot pan

mat

wood surface

Heat energy travels easily through a conductor...

...but hardly at all through an insulator.

Aluminium is another good conductor. You can use it to speed up the cooking of baked potatoes in the oven.

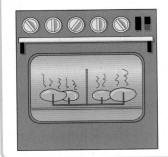

It takes a long time for baked potatoes to cook through to the middle.

Using aluminium spikes, they cook through in half the time.

3 Which is the better conductor of heat, metal or plastic?

4 Explain why pans used for cooking often have a metal base but a plastic handle.

5 Name two metals that are good heat conductors.

6 Suggest a reason why joints of meat with a bone in can take less time to roast than the same meat that has had the bone taken out.

Air is a very poor conductor

The particles in a gas are spread out. They fly about and hit each other occasionally, but most of the time they are not connected. Air is a gas. This makes air a very poor conductor because the particles cannot pass the heat energy on easily.

We use air as a good insulator in lots of ways. Lots of layers of clothes keep you warmer in winter than one thick garment. This is because each layer traps some air. The layer of air acts as an insulator. Polystyrene cups made to keep drinks hot have tiny bubbles of air trapped in their walls.

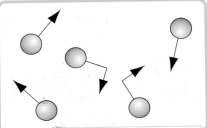

The particles in a gas move about and collide with each other. There are far fewer particles in each cubic centimetre than there are in a solid or a liquid. So gases are poor thermal conductors.

plastic

small bubble of trapped air

Foam plastic insulation

fibre

small 'pocket' of trapped air

Clothing fibre insulation

7 How are the particles in a gas arranged?

8 What is it about the arrangement of particles in a gas that makes it a poor conductor of heat?

9 How do clothes make use of air to keep the heat in?

Conduction makes some things feel cold

Sometimes, two things at the same temperature feel like they are at different temperatures when you touch them. An example of this happens when you touch the handlebars and the seat of a bike.

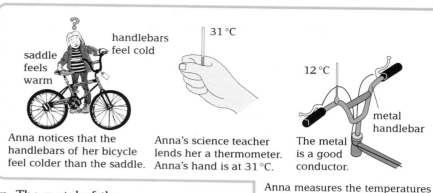

Anna notices that the handlebars of her bicycle feel colder than the saddle.

Anna's science teacher lends her a thermometer. Anna's hand is at 31 °C.

The metal is a good conductor.

This happens because of conduction. The metal of the handlebars is a good conductor. It is colder than your hand so heat energy flows quickly out of your hand when you touch the metal. The flow of heat energy makes your hand feel cold. The plastic seat is not such a good conductor so it feels a lot warmer when you touch it. This is because the heat energy does not flow out of your hand so quickly.

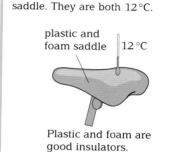

Anna measures the temperatures of the handlebars and the saddle. They are both 12 °C.

Plastic and foam are good insulators.

10 Which feels colder when you touch it, the handlebar or the saddle? Give a reason for your answer.

11 If you had to get a spade from the garden shed on a frosty day, would it be better to get hold of the wooden part or the metal part? Give a reason for your answer.

81.4 Moving the heat energy in liquids and gases

You can get heat energy to move through liquids and gases, but it happens in a different way to the conduction of heat in solids.

Boiling a kettle

Look at the pictures of a kettle.

- The heating element of a kettle heats the water around it.

- The particles in the hot water move faster and move further apart.

- The hot water is less dense than the cold water around it. So the hot water rises up through the cold water.

- Cold water replaces the hot water around the heating element and starts to heat up.

- The water cycles around the kettle until it boils.

This is called **convection**.

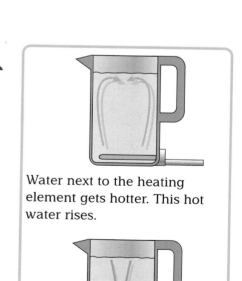

Water next to the heating element gets hotter. This hot water rises.

Colder water then falls down to take its place.

Gases and liquids are both fluids. So the same idea applies to the air in a room. Hot air is less dense than cold air, so it rises up from around the wall heater. The cold air moves in to replace it. The cycle of air is known as a <u>convection current</u>. Heat transfers in this way in liquids and gases – because they are fluids, they can flow.

You can see the convection currents in water by using a dye. You can see the effect of convection currents in air with a spiral made of thin paper. It turns as hot air rises past it.

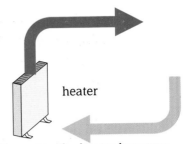
heater

Air next to the heater becomes hotter. This hot air rises. Colder air then falls to take its place.

1 Which is denser, hot water or cold water?

2 What is the name for the current that forms when hot water floats upwards and cold water sinks?

3 What happens to the particles in water when the temperature increases?

4 How does the increase in temperature of water affect the density of the water?

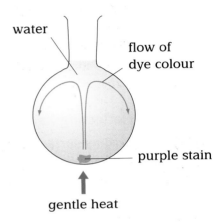
water

flow of dye colour

purple stain

gentle heat

More convection currents

Convection currents also occur in nature. Farm buildings, ploughed fields and tarmac warm the air so convection currents called thermals rise above them. Glider pilots use them to gain height.

5 What is the name for the convection currents used by glider pilots to gain height?

6 Describe how convection currents move inside a fridge.

Hint: the cooling unit is at the top.

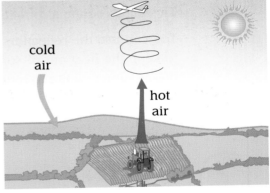
cold air

hot air

A lava lamp also uses convection. The bulb at the bottom of the lamp heats the coloured wax inside. The hot wax rises upwards because it is less dense than the liquid. The wax cools when it gets to the top of the lamp and sinks back down. It gets heated again at the bottom and the cycle continues.

7 Sea breezes often blow from the sea towards the land during the day. At night they often blow from the land towards the sea. Find out why this happens.

81.5 How energy travels through space

During the daytime, heat energy reaches the Earth's surface from the Sun. The energy has taken about 8 minutes to travel across 150 million kilometres of empty space. It does not happen by conduction or convection, because there is nothing between the Sun and the Earth to allow conduction or convection to happen. This method of heat transfer is called **radiation**. We say that the Sun radiates heat energy in the same way that it radiates light.

 1 How is the energy from the Sun carried to the Earth?

 2 Through what can heat transfer by radiation happen while heat transfer by conduction and convection cannot?

Reflecting heat radiation

A shiny surface reflects heat radiation just like it reflects light. You can feel this effect if you hold your hand in front of a spotlight bulb in a reading light and compare it to an ordinary bulb at the same distance.

The spotlight bulb has a shiny coating to reflect more light forwards. The shiny coating also reflects radiated heat energy.

You can use the reflection from a shiny or light-coloured surface to keep the heat out of some things. Houses in hot countries are often painted white to reflect the heat radiation and keep the building a bit cooler. Fridges and freezers are usually shiny white to reflect heat radiation. Petrol storage tanks at refineries usually have shiny walls to reflect the heat radiation from the Sun.

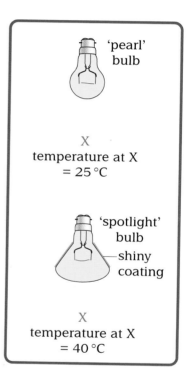

'pearl' bulb

X
temperature at X
= 25 °C

'spotlight' bulb
shiny coating

X
temperature at X
= 40 °C

 3 What can a shiny or light-coloured surface do to heat radiation?
4 Why are some objects coloured white or given shiny surfaces to keep them cool?

 5 How might spotlight bulbs be used in restaurants to keep plates of food hot until they are taken out and served?

8I.6 Keeping warm

Keeping the house warm

A three-bedroom house in Britain can cost as much as £15 a week to keep warm. You can reduce this by half if you control the heat loss to the outside air. This diagram shows how much energy you can lose every second from a house on a winter's day. The total number of joules shown on the diagram would be enough to bring 2 litres of cold water to the boil in about one minute!

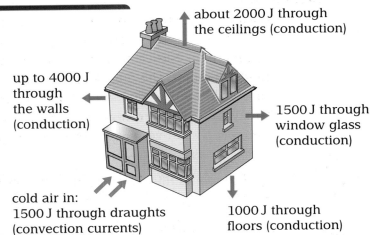

about 2000 J through the ceilings (conduction)

up to 4000 J through the walls (conduction)

1500 J through window glass (conduction)

cold air in: 1500 J through draughts (convection currents)

1000 J through floors (conduction)

One of the cheapest things you can do is to insulate your loft with layers of glass fibre. Convection currents cause the hot air to rise up inside your house. The glass fibre traps air, which acts as a good insulator and reduces heat loss by conduction though the roof. It costs about £300 to insulate a loft. In a year you could save about £150 on your heating bills.

Draught excluders only cost a few pounds to fit and they can save about £50 in a year. Double glazing is more expensive. It would probably take over ten years for someone to save enough to pay for it on their heating bills. Double glazing works by trapping a layer of air between two sheets of glass. The air acts as an insulator. Apart from reducing heat loss, it also reduces the level of sound coming in from outside. Many people have double glazing fitted because it makes it quieter inside the house.

The radiated heat from the back of a radiator can be reflected back into the room by a shiny plastic sheet on the wall. Sometimes the walls of a house are made of two layers of brick with plastic foam between them. This is known as cavity wall insulation.

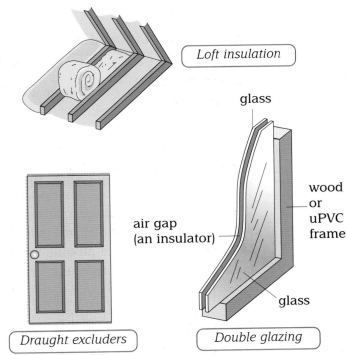

Loft insulation

glass

air gap (an insulator)

wood or uPVC frame

glass

Draught excluders

Double glazing

1 Describe <u>two</u> ways of reducing heat loss from your house. Explain how <u>one</u> of these works.

2 Why might someone have double glazing fitted if they only plan to live in the house for a few years? Suggest several different reasons.

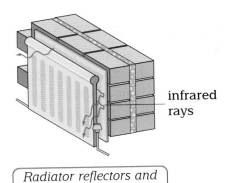

infrared rays

Radiator reflectors and cavity wall insulation

The Thermos flask

A Thermos flask keeps hot things hot and cold things cold. Its walls are designed to prevent heat energy passing through them.

There are no particles in a vacuum so conduction and convection cannot happen. The only way that heat energy can cross a vacuum is by radiation. A shiny surface is a good reflector of radiation. The wall reflects back the small amount that reaches it. This means that very little radiated heat crosses the vacuum and escapes.

The stopper is filled with plastic foam, which contains trapped air to make it a poor conductor. The stopper also stops convection currents carrying heat out of the top of the flask.

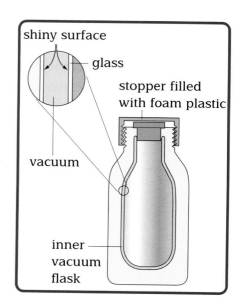

shiny surface

glass

stopper filled with foam plastic

vacuum

inner vacuum flask

3 What is a vacuum?

4 What is the only method of heat transfer that can cross a vacuum? Give a reason for your answer.

5 Find out who James Dewar was and what his connection to the Thermos flask is.

81.7 Changing between solid, liquid and gas

When you want to change a solid to a liquid or a liquid to a gas, you have to heat the solid or liquid up to get its particles moving faster. You also need to provide some extra energy so the particles can separate from each other.

Monitoring the temperature

A beaker containing 200 g of crushed ice is taken from a freezer at −15 °C. It is heated until the ice has melted and warmed up to about 60 °C. The temperature is logged at intervals of time as the ice is melting. A computer plots a graph of temperature against time.

The first section of the graph shows the temperature rise while the ice warms up. Once it reaches 0 °C the temperature stays the same while the ice melts. This happens because the heat energy being supplied is used to get the particles to break loose from each other rather than go any faster.

The water is changing from a solid to a liquid. The temperature where a solid changes into a liquid or a liquid changes into a solid is called its **melting point**. Once all the ice has melted the heat energy starts to make the particles move faster and the temperature starts to rise again.

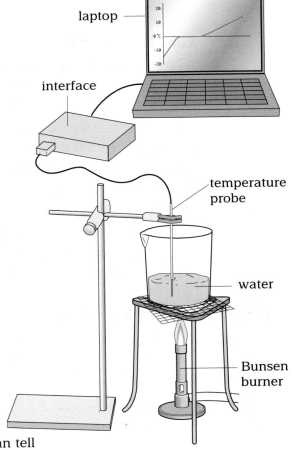

laptop

interface

temperature probe

water

Bunsen burner

1   What is happening to the ice where the temperature stays the same on the graph?

2   What does the energy supplied to the particles in the melting ice do while the temperature stays the same?

3   What happens to the temperature of the water once all the ice has melted? Give a reason for your answer in terms of what is happening to the particles.

About melting points

Different substances have different melting points. You can tell where the melting point is by plotting a graph of the temperature as something melts. The melting point is the temperature where the graph flattens out while the particles break free of each other. You can also find the melting point from a <u>cooling curve</u>. A cooling curve is the same type of graph in reverse, where you cool the liquid down into a solid and plot its temperature. This is the type of graph you get when a liquid cools and changes to a solid.

4   At what temperature does the liquid start changing to a solid?

5   How long does it take for the liquid to change into a solid, from the moment it starts to solidify?

6   How do you think the shape of the graph would change if the experiment was repeated in much colder surroundings?

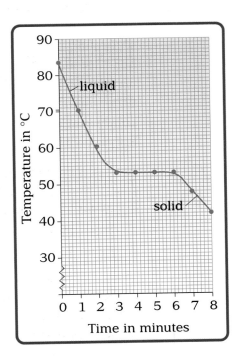

Evaporation, boiling and condensation

As you heat up water, some of the faster particles start to escape from the surface. We call this **evaporation**. Evaporation happens at all temperatures. You can see this on a cold day after it has rained. Even though it takes a while, eventually the roads and pavements will dry out by evaporation. On a hot summer's day the roads and pavements dry out much more quickly. Sometimes you can even see steam in the air above them.

When you heat water so that bubbles of evaporated water form everywhere in the body of the water, we say the water is boiling. The temperature at which a liquid boils is called its **boiling point**.

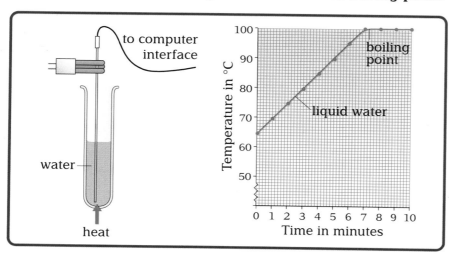

Once water boils, the heat energy being supplied to it goes into separating the particles to form a gas. This means steam at 100 °C has a lot more energy than water at 100 °C. A scald from boiling water is pretty bad but a scald from steam is a lot worse! If you cool water vapour or steam down it changes back to water. We call this **condensation**. The steam that emerges from a kettle or a steam iron is visible because it is beginning to condense.

7   What effect causes pavements to dry after it rains?

8   What is the name for the effect when bubbles of vapour form all the way through a body of water?

9   What is condensation?

10 Why can a scald from steam be worse than a scald from boiling water?

11 Find out who James Watt was. What was his connection with steam?

You should now understand the key words and key ideas shown below.

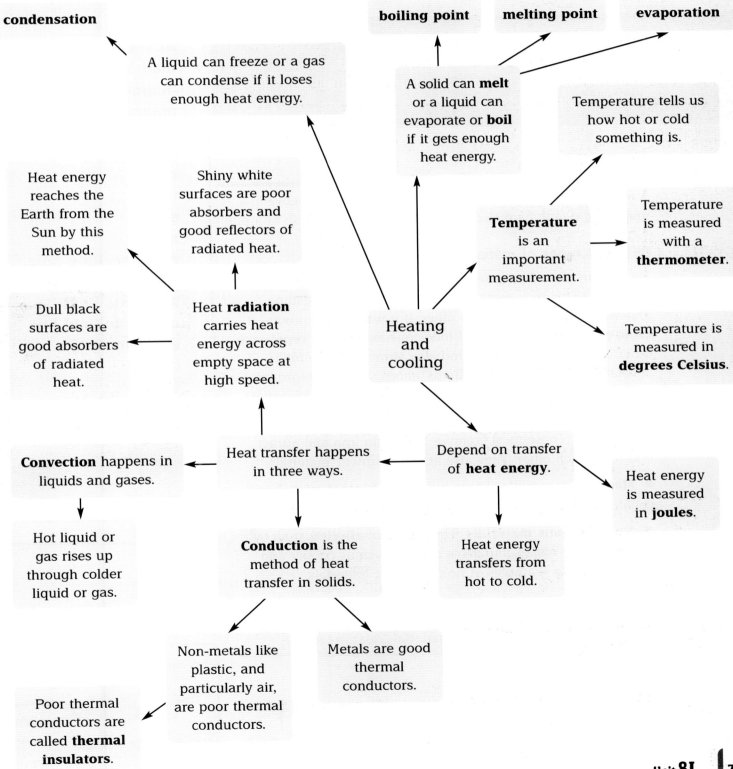

condensation

A liquid can freeze or a gas can condense if it loses enough heat energy.

boiling point   **melting point**   **evaporation**

A solid can **melt** or a liquid can evaporate or **boil** if it gets enough heat energy.

Temperature tells us how hot or cold something is.

Heat energy reaches the Earth from the Sun by this method.

Shiny white surfaces are poor absorbers and good reflectors of radiated heat.

Temperature is an important measurement.

Temperature is measured with a **thermometer**.

Dull black surfaces are good absorbers of radiated heat.

Heat **radiation** carries heat energy across empty space at high speed.

Heating and cooling

Temperature is measured in **degrees Celsius**.

Convection happens in liquids and gases.

Heat transfer happens in three ways.

Depend on transfer of **heat energy**.

Heat energy is measured in **joules**.

Hot liquid or gas rises up through colder liquid or gas.

Conduction is the method of heat transfer in solids.

Heat energy transfers from hot to cold.

Poor thermal conductors are called **thermal insulators**.

Non-metals like plastic, and particularly air, are poor thermal conductors.

Metals are good thermal conductors.

Magnets and electromagnets

In this unit we shall be studying magnets and electromagnets, what they can do and how to make them, and familiar objects that use them. We shall learn about magnetic fields and how to plot them.

KEY WORDS
magnetic force
magnets
magnetic materials
non-magnetic materials
attract
repel
iron
steel
nickel
north-seeking pole
south-seeking pole
magnetic field
magnetic field line
electromagnets
coil
core
relay

8J.1 Magnetic forces

A **magnetic force** exists between two magnets and between a magnet and any magnetic material. This can be a push or a pull.

Different types of materials

Many years ago, the Ancient Greeks discovered a rock called lodestone. This rock could pull another lump of lodestone towards it. They **attract** each other. If it was turned around it could push the other lump of lodestone away. They **repel** each other. Lodestones in the ground also attracted some other substances. They made shepherds' shoes stick to the ground by attracting the iron tacks in their soles. The Greeks found that they could separate materials into three groups:

● **Magnets** These most commonly contain iron and attract and repel each other. They also attract magnetic materials.

● **Magnetic materials** These include **iron**, **steel**, **nickel** and cobalt. They are attracted to magnets but not to each other.

● **Non-magnetic materials** These are not affected at all by magnets. Non-metals and some metals, such as copper and aluminium, are examples of non-magnetic materials.

?
1 What <u>three</u> groups did the Greeks put materials into?
2 What happens to magnetic materials near magnets?

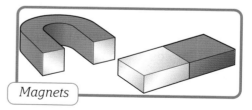
Magnets

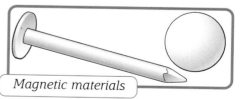
Magnetic materials

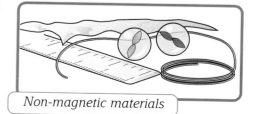
Non-magnetic materials

Magnetic attraction

Magnets only attract magnets and magnetic materials. Steel is a magnetic material but aluminium is not, so magnets are used to sort aluminium cans from steel cans for recycling. The steel cans are attracted to the magnet, leaving the non-magnetic aluminium cans behind.

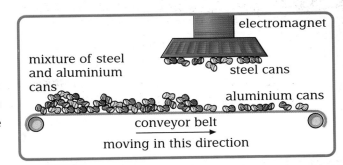

4 **a** Are steel cans magnetic or non-magnetic?

b Are aluminium cans magnetic or non-magnetic?

5 When the magnet is used, explain whether:

a the steel cans are attracted to it or left behind;

b the aluminium cans are attracted to it or left behind.

What magnetic forces pass through

Fridge magnets can hold pieces of paper or thin plastic to a painted fridge door.

A strong magnet held one side of your hand can move a magnetic object on the other side. The magnetic force passes through non-magnetic materials like paper, plastic, paint, skin and bone.

Dangle a paperclip near a magnet and the magnet will attract it. Now put a sheet of iron in the gap between the magnet and the paperclip. The magnet does not attract the paperclip as much because the iron partially stops the magnetic force passing through. Magnetic materials do not let magnetic forces pass through.

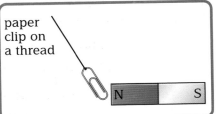
paper clip on a thread

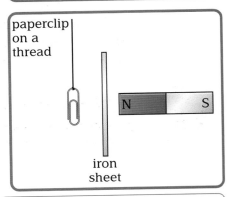
paperclip on a thread

iron sheet

The iron sheet stops the magnet from attracting the paperclip.

6 What type of material:

a lets magnetic forces pass through it;

b will not let magnetic forces pass through it?

7 Would magnetic forces pass through:

a aluminium; **b** steel?

8 How would each of these materials behave near a magnet?

a nickel **b** plastic **c** iron

Poles of a magnet

Early explorers discovered that when a magnet could move freely, it always came to rest with one end pointing towards the Earth's north. This is called the **north-seeking pole** or north pole for short. The other end point towards the Earth's south. This is called the **south-seeking pole** or south sole for short. The explorers used this to make a compass, which contains a magnet that is free to spin, to find their way in unknown places.

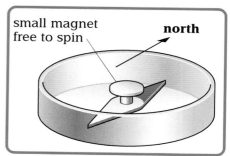

small magnet free to spin

north

8 What are the names given to the two ends of a magnet?

9 What happens when a magnet is left to move freely?

How the poles of a magnet behave

Magnets attract or repel other magnets. Some toy trains use magnets to hold the carriages together. Put the carriages facing the wrong way and they push each other apart. Two south poles, or two north poles will repel each other. However, magnets attract each other if a north pole and a south pole face each other. The magnetic force is strongest at the poles of a magnet.

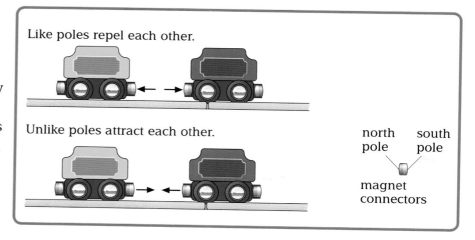

Like poles repel each other.

Unlike poles attract each other.

north pole   south pole

magnet connectors

10 Are these magnets attracting or repelling each other?

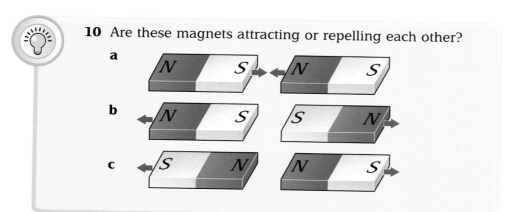

a

b

c

11 Does a compass always tell you which way is north? Find out about places where the needle of a compass does not point to north and explain why.

8J.2 Magnetic fields

There is an area around any magnet where that magnet would have an effect on a magnetic material. We call this area the **magnetic field**.

The shape of magnetic fields

Iron filings around a magnet arrange themselves into a pattern which shows the shape of the magnetic field around it.

You can use compasses to plot the direction of the magnetic field around a magnet.

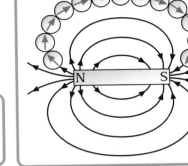

small compasses

Put a piece of card on top of the magnet.

Sprinkle iron filings as evenly as you can.

Tap the card with your finger.

1   What can you use to show someone where the magnetic field is around a magnet?

2   Draw a diagram to show the shape of the magnetic field around a bar magnet.

3   Use your diagram to show the direction of the magnetic field.

The strength of magnetic fields

The two diagrams show the magnetic field around a strong magnet and a weak magnet. Where the magnetic force is stronger, the field is drawn with more lines of force. Although the fields are the same shape, there are more lines of force drawn around the stronger magnet.

4   Where is the magnetic field of a magnet strongest?

5   What can you say about the number of lines of force for each magnet in the diagrams?

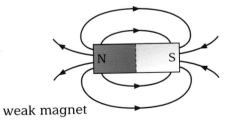

weak magnet

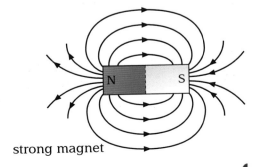

strong magnet

The Earth's magnetic field

A compass is used to help you find your way. This works because the Earth behaves as if it had a giant magnet inside it. This means that the Earth has a magnetic field. The magnet in the compass lines up with the Earth's magnetic field so that you can always tell which direction you are facing. In 1600, William Gilbert published work that described the Earth as a great spherical magnet. He had carried out experiments to back up his claim. He was a physician who worked for Queen Elizabeth I.

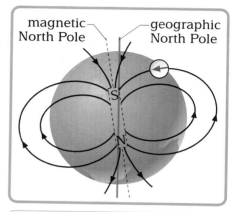

The imaginary magnet which could produce the Earth's **magnetic field lines**. Its south pole points towards the Arctic and its north pole points towards the Antarctic.

6   What do you use a compass for?
7   What do we call the area around a magnet?

8   How can you tell that the Earth has a magnetic field?

9   If you placed a compass between two magnets, how could you tell which magnet was the stronger?

8J.3   Making and using magnets

You can make your own magnet using a magnet and an iron nail. Stroke the iron nail several times with one end of the magnet, and the iron becomes a magnet too. The iron will not stay magnetic for ever – it will lose its magnetism gradually. You can make temporary magnets in this way using any of the magnetic materials.

1   What do you need to make a magnet?

2   Name <u>three</u> materials that you can turn into a magnet by stroking them with another magnet.

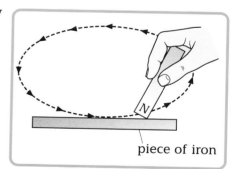
piece of iron

Using magnets

Magnets can be used to keep cupboard and fridge doors closed. A fridge door has a magnetic strip right around the door which keeps the door tightly closed.

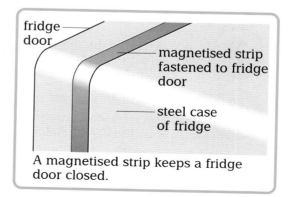
fridge door

magnetised strip fastened to fridge door

steel case of fridge

A magnetised strip keeps a fridge door closed.

Magnetic trains use magnets to float the train above the rail. This reduces friction and so the train can travel faster. The first design used magnets on the bottom of the train, which were repelled by magnetic forces in the rail.

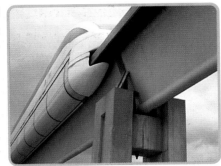

3 How can you arrange two magnets so that they repel each other instead of attracting each other? Give <u>two</u> methods.

The diagram shows another design. The rail's magnets hang below the rail and are attracted upwards, lifting the train up to 5cm above the rail.

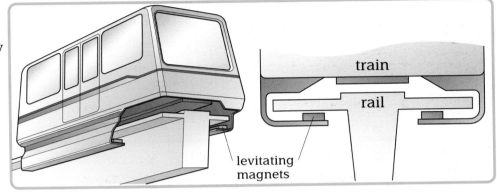
train
rail
levitating magnets

4 Suggest a material that the rails could be made from.

Magnetic tape contains many tiny magnetic particles. Information is stored on the tape when the particles are magnetised into different patterns. Because there are so many particles, the amount of information that can be stored is huge. Tape cassettes contain a length of magnetic tape, which is magnetised when a recording is made. This stores the information so the sound can be played back later.

Before recording	After recording

When the information is recorded on the magnetic strip, the magnetic particles line up into a pattern.

Credit cards also have a magnetic strip, which stores information. Any magnets near to the magnetic strip can rearrange the particles, changing the information held.

Computers store information on floppy disks when the iron particles on the disks are magnetised into different patterns.

5 How does magnetic tape store information?

6 Why do you think it is important to keep credit cards and floppy disks away from strong magnets?

7 Stroking with a magnet is not the only way to turn a magnetic material into a magnet. Research another method.

8J.4 Making and using electromagnets

When an electric current flows through a wire, the wire behaves like a weak magnet. The wire can be made from any type of metal. It doesn't have to be a magnetic material. You can use compasses around the wire to show its magnetic field. Magnets made using electricity are called **electromagnets**.

Electromagnets are very useful because they can be switched on and off. If you turn the current off, the electromagnet loses its magnetism. Switch the current on again and the magnet is switched back on.

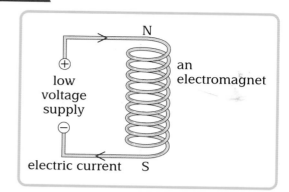

1 How can you make an electromagnet?

2 What can you use to show the magnetic field around an electromagnet?

How to make electromagnets stronger

Some electromagnets are so weak that they cannot even pick up a paperclip. Others are strong enough to pick up a car! You can change the strength of the magnet by changing the size of the current – a larger current creates a stronger electromagnet. To make an even stronger electromagnet, you need to wind the wire into a **coil** and place a piece of iron inside the coil of wire. This piece of iron is called the **core**. It is important to choose the right material to make an electromagnet, however. Some magnetic materials, like iron, lose their magnetism when the current is switched off. These are called <u>soft</u> magnetic materials. Steel stays magnetised. It is called a <u>hard</u> magnetic material.

3 What are <u>three</u> ways to make an electromagnet stronger?

4 Give <u>one</u> useful difference between electromagnets and permanent magnets.

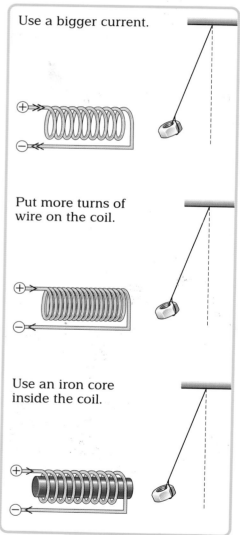

Use a bigger current.

Put more turns of wire on the coil.

Use an iron core inside the coil.

Ways to make an electromagnet stronger.

How do electromagnets work?

Wires carrying an electric current produce a magnetic field around them. If the wire is coiled, the electromagnetic field pattern is similar to that of a bar magnet. If an iron core is then placed inside the coil, the iron is magnetised. This is why the strength of an electromagnet is increased when an iron core is used.

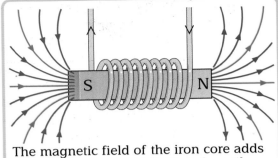

The magnetic field of the iron core adds itself to the magnetic field of the coil.

 5 Why is an electromagnet stronger if it has an iron core?

 6 What other materials would be good for making the core, so that the electromagnet is strong?

 7 Find out what magnetic domains are.

Using electromagnets

Cranes in scrapyards use electromagnets to move old cars around. Switching the current on creates an electromagnet that is strong enough to lift the cars, which contain iron and steel. When a car has been moved to the correct place, the current is switched off. This turns off the electromagnet and the car is left in its new position.

The electromagnet in the crane lifts a scrap car.

When the crane driver switches off the current, the car falls.

 8 Why are the cars attracted to the electromagnet?

 9 How is the electromagnet switched on and off in a crane?

Some doorbells use electromagnets. When a switch is pressed, the circuit is complete and a current flows through the electromagnet. The electromagnet attracts a springy metal strip holding the hammer. When the hammer moves and hits the gong, it breaks the circuit. The current stops flowing, the electromagnet turns off and the metal strip moves back, completing the circuit. This starts the cycle once again.

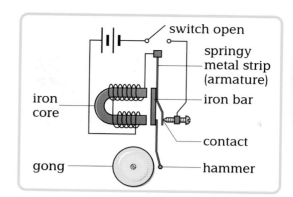

 10 In a doorbell, what is attracted to the electromagnet?

 11 How is the electromagnet switched off?

Relays

Relays use the current from one circuit to control the current in another circuit. When the first circuit is switched on, an electromagnet becomes magnetised, attracting the iron switch (called an armature) in the other circuit. The movement of the armature completes the second circuit and this allows a current to flow in the second circuit. The diagram shows a relay circuit that controls a light by remote control.

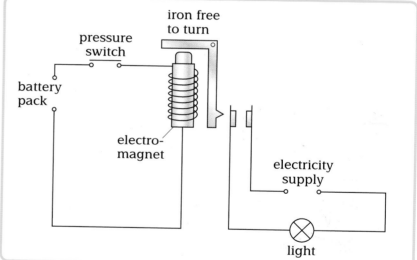

This circuit controls a light that switches on if someone steps on the pressure switch.

Car starter motors use relays. A small current flows in one circuit when the key is turned. This turns on the starter motor circuit, which uses a very large current. This is a safe way to switch on a large current.

 12 Why is a relay switch used with a car starter motor?

 13 Describe how the relay in the diagram switches on the light when the pressure switch is pressed.

You should now understand the key words and key ideas shown below.

Key words

magnetic force	magnet	magnetic material	non-magnetic material
attract	repel	nickel	steel
north-seeking pole	south-seeking pole	magnetic field	magnetic field line
electromagnets	core	coil	relay

Key ideas

Magnets create a **magnetic force** between one another and between themselves and magnetic materials.

Magnets can **attract** and **repel** one another. They also attract magnetic materials.

Magnetic materials are attracted to magnets but not to each other. Examples of magnetic materials are; iron, **steel** and **nickel**.

Non-magnetic materials are not affected at all by magnets.

The magnetic force passes through non-magnetic materials but not through magnetic materials.

The ends of magnets are called poles. The **south-seeking pole** points south and the **north-seeking pole** points north.

A north-seeking pole and a south-seeking pole attract each other, but two south-seeking poles or two north-seeking poles repel each other.

The area around magnets is called the **magnetic field**. **Magnetic field lines** can be plotted with a compass.

The direction of the magnetic field goes from the magnet's north pole to its south pole.

Stronger magnets are represented by showing more lines of force around them.

The Earth behaves as if it had a giant magnet inside it.

The magnet in a compass lines up with the Earth's magnetic field.

You can make your own magnet by stroking an iron nail with one end of a magnet.

When an electric current flows through a wire, the wire behaves like a weak magnet.

Magnets made using electricity are called **electromagnets**. These contain a **core**, usually of iron, and a **coil** of wire which carries an electric current.

Electromagnets are very useful because they can be switched on and off.

You can change the strength of an electromagnet by changing the size of the current, coiling the wire or placing a piece of iron inside the coil of wire.

Relay switches use the current from one circuit to switch on the current in another circuit.

A relay switch has an electro-magnet in one circuit next to an iron switch in the other circuit.

8K

Light

In this unit we shall study light and learn how it behaves when it hits things and how colours are produced from white light. We shall also learn how light bounces off mirrors and how we can make light bend.

KEY WORDS

light source
ray
transmitted
reflected
absorbed
transparent
translucent
opaque
luminous
non-luminous
normal
image
object
refraction
prism
spectrum

8K.1 Where light comes from and how it travels

Light comes from sources

A **light source** is anything that produces light. The Sun is our main light source. There are places where light from the Sun does not reach, like windowless rooms or down mine shafts. Light from the Sun also fades towards the end of the day. Since prehistoric times humans have used other light sources to help them see when it is dark.

Until about 1900 most of our extra light sources involved burning something. Nearly all the extra light sources we use today, such as light bulbs, involve electricity. Electricity is more convenient. For example, you can store the energy for it in cells and batteries and move it from place to place along wires.

Electric light sources can be switched on and off instantly. Electric light sources are also safer than candles and oil lamps because they do not have flames in them, so there is less risk of starting a fire.

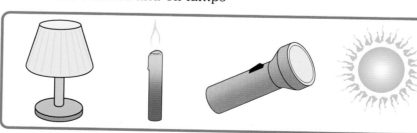

1 What is meant by a light source? Give <u>three</u> examples.
2 What is our main source of light?

Examples of light sources

3 Why is electricity more useful than candle wax or oil to power a light source? Give <u>four</u> reasons.

82 Unit **8K**

Light travels in straight lines

One of the earliest experiments with light looked like this.

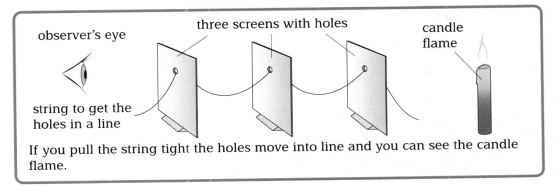

observer's eye

three screens with holes

candle flame

string to get the holes in a line

If you pull the string tight the holes move into line and you can see the candle flame.

The experiment shows that light travels in straight lines. Because of this we use straight lines with arrows to represent light. We call each line a **ray**. A light ray shows you the path that the light follows. A diagram that uses rays to show what light does is called a <u>ray diagram</u>.

The ray diagram shows how a torch and a pencil can be used to make a shadow. The light cannot go through the pencil. Because light travels in straight lines it cannot go round the pencil. That is why the pencil casts a shadow when it is put in front of the torch.

When you draw a ray diagram you just draw the main rays. You usually include the rays at the edges. You draw the rays as straight lines with arrows on them to show the direction the light travels in. The arrow always points away from the light source to show the direction.

The rays from the torch are spreading out. The light from the Sun is spreading out all over space. Because the Earth is so small compared to its distance from the Sun, the Sun's light rays reach us in a parallel beam.

This ray diagram shows how light rays from the Sun form a shadow of a tree.

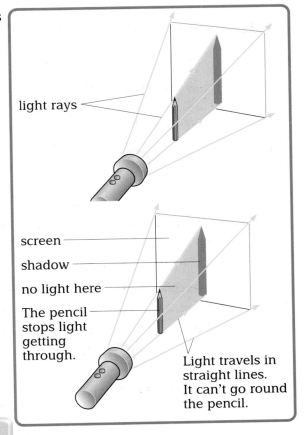

light rays

screen

shadow

no light here

The pencil stops light getting through.

Light travels in straight lines. It can't go round the pencil.

4 What is a light ray?

5 Why is a light ray drawn as a straight line?

6 Which property of light makes a pencil cast a shadow when it is held in front of a light source?

light from Sun

Light gets there straight away

If you go to watch a cricket match, you see the ball being hit but you hear the sound a short time later. This happens because light travels at an incredibly high speed and seems to reach you straight away. Sound travels about a million times slower and takes a fraction of a second to reach you. The first attempt to measure how fast light travels was by an Italian called Galileo Galilei in 1600. He tried uncovering a lantern and timing how long the light took to travel a few miles to another person. His idea did not work because the smallest time he could estimate was about a tenth of a second. The time light actually took was only a few millionths of a second!

Scientists made the first really accurate measurements of the speed of light about 150 years ago using mirrors spinning very fast. These experiments were improved and changed, and we now know that light travels 300 000 000 metres in one second.

> Mama mia! I did not expect that! His light came on straight away. The speed of light is too quick for me to measure.

Distance	Time for light to travel that distance
From a light in the ceiling to the edge of a room in a house (about 3 m)	1 one hundred millionth of a second
From a lighthouse to a ship 20 miles away	1 ten thousandth of a second
From the Sun to the Earth (150 000 000 km)	500 seconds (about $8\frac{1}{2}$ minutes)
From the Sun to the edge of the Solar System (Pluto is about 5 900 000 000 km from the Sun)	About 20 000 seconds which is about $5\frac{1}{2}$ hours!
From the nearest star (Proxima Centauri) to us (about 40 400 000 000 000 km)	135 000 000 seconds, which is about $4\frac{1}{4}$ years!
From the edge of the observable universe to us (about 100 000 000 000 000 000 000 000 km)	About 10 000 million years!

7 Why can you see someone hit a ball before you hear the sound produced when you are a few hundred metres away?

8 Why does the light seem to fill a room instantly when you switch an electric light on?

9 If the Sun suddenly went out one day, how long would it be until we noticed?

10 Find out what a light year is and why it is used to measure distances in space.

8K.2 Light hitting objects

When light hits something it can do one of three things:

- go through (be **transmitted**);
- bounce back (be **reflected**);
- stay inside and heat up the object (be **absorbed**).

Going straight through

Some substances let light go straight through them. Glass, water, air and some types of plastic are good examples. We say these substances are **transparent**.

1 What is a transparent substance?
2 Give two examples of transparent substances and where they might be used.

3 List some advantages and disadvantages of glass as a substance for windows.

Letting the light through but breaking it up

Sometimes you want to let the light through, but you do not want anyone to be able to see through. We use a **translucent** substance to break the light up. Examples in the home are:

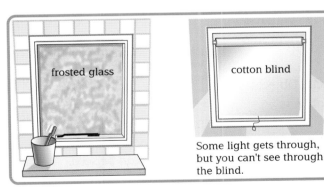
frosted glass

cotton blind

Some light gets through, but you can't see through the blind.

- frosted glass;
- plastic or glass with very detailed patterns on;
- sheets of white cotton;

- 'pearl' light bulbs give an even glow compared with the glaring light you get from a clear bulb.

Clouds are translucent. The Sun's light is scattered when it comes through them. That is why there are no shadows on a cloudy day even though it is still light.

4 What is a translucent substance?
5 Give <u>three</u> examples of where a translucent substance might be useful.
6 What do clouds do to the Sun's light rays?

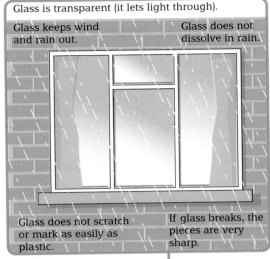
Glass is transparent (it lets light through).

Glass keeps wind and rain out.

Glass does not dissolve in rain.

Glass does not scratch or mark as easily as plastic.

If glass breaks, the pieces are very sharp.

A car windscreen is transparent.

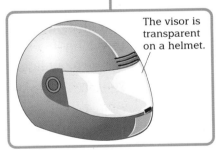
The visor is transparent on a helmet.

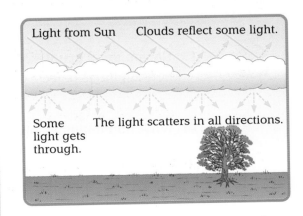
Light from Sun   Clouds reflect some light.

Some light gets through.   The light scatters in all directions.

Unit **8K** | 85

Stopping the light

Some substances stop light going through them. We say that a substance that stops light is **opaque**. Metal and wood are opaque substances. Some types of plastic are opaque.

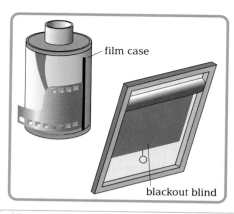

film case

blackout blind

You must use an opaque substance for the case of a photographic film or the light will spoil it. The windows in a roof can be fitted with opaque blinds to shut sunlight out completely.

7 What is an opaque substance?

8 Give <u>two</u> examples of where an opaque substance might be useful.

Bouncing off an opaque surface

Pale or white things reflect most of the light that falls on them. Black and dark things absorb most of the light that falls on them.

9 Opaque substances of which colours reflect most of the light that falls on them?

10 What can cyclists and pedestrians do to make sure that they are visible and safe at night?

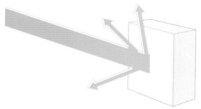

White things and pale things reflect most of the light that falls on them.

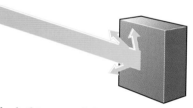

Black things and dark things reflect very little of the light that falls on them. They absorb most of the light.

Light entering your eye

You see an object when light from it enters your eye. For objects that give out light, like a light bulb, that usually means the light is travelling in a straight line from it to your eye. For objects that do not give out light, you see them when light reflects off them into your eye.

Objects that give out light are called **luminous** objects. Objects that do not give out light are called **non-luminous** objects.

11 What happens for you to see a luminous object?

12 What happens for you to see a non-luminous object?

13 Do you think that the Moon is a luminous or a non-luminous object? Give a reason for your answer.

14 What non-luminous objects can be seen from the Earth in the night sky? Can any of them be seen in the daytime? Give reasons for your answer.

The only luminous object is the light bulb. When it is not on then none of the objects in the room can be seen.

8K.3 Mirrors

Mirrors reflect light without scattering it. This makes them very useful in many situations. A mirror reflects nearly all of the light that falls on it. The same is true of a piece of white paper, but you cannot see your face in a piece of paper.

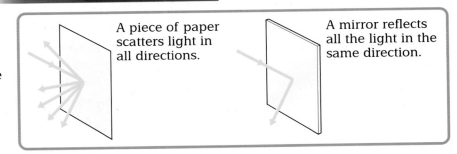

A piece of paper scatters light in all directions.

A mirror reflects all the light in the same direction.

A mirror reflects a ray of light at the same angle as it strikes it. We measure the angle of the light hitting and leaving the mirror from a reference line called the **normal**. The normal is a line drawn at 90° to the surface of the mirror.

The light hitting the mirror is called the incident ray. The light leaving the mirror is called the reflected ray. You can use mirrors to see things you could not normally look at.

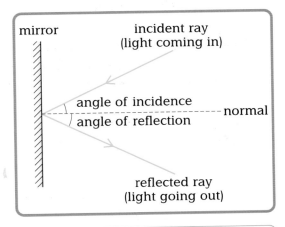

mirror
incident ray (light coming in)
angle of incidence
angle of reflection
normal
reflected ray (light going out)

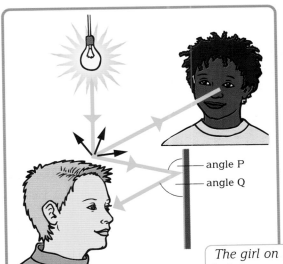

angle P

angle Q

Angle A and angle B are equal. The mirror reflects a beam at the same angle it strikes the mirror.

The girl on the right can see the boy's hair because light bounces off the hair and enters her eye. The boy can see his own hair because light from it bounces off the mirror and then enters his eye.

Mirrors are sometimes used to help drivers 'see round corners'.

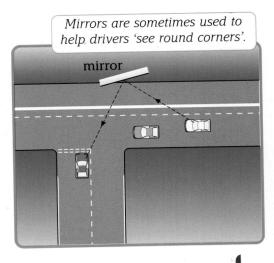

mirror

1   What is the difference between light bouncing off a piece of paper and light bouncing off a mirror?

2   What rule does light obey when it bounces off a mirror? Draw a diagram to show this.

3   Look at the road diagram. Draw a diagram to show where you would put a second mirror so that the driver of the blue car could see round the corner to the left.

Looking in a flat mirror

A flat mirror is also known as a <u>plane</u> mirror. When you look into a mirror you see an **image** of your face. A mirror image is a copy of something that you see when light has had its direction changed. The light from your face has had its direction changed when it bounced off the mirror. The reflected light seems to come out of the mirror and you see an image of your face in the mirror. Because of the way light reflects off a flat mirror the image of your face follows certain rules.

 you    mirror    your image

4 How does the size of the image compare with the size of the object when you look at something in a plane mirror?

5 What happens to writing when you look at it in a mirror? Find an example of where this effect is used.

6 What are the important differences between looking at a photograph of your face and looking at yourself in a mirror?

RULE 1 The image is the same size. Your face does not look bigger or smaller.

RULE 2 Your reflection looks as if it is as far into the mirror as your face is in front of the mirror.

RULE 3 We call the thing that the light comes from the **object**. In the diagram shown here the real face is the object. The image is the opposite way around to the object.

Using two mirrors to see over the top of things

If you want to see over the top of something, you can use two mirrors in an instrument called a <u>periscope</u>. It is made from two mirrors in a tube. The light enters the periscope, reflects off the first mirror at the top, and travels down to the bottom mirror. Then the light is reflected into your eye. Periscopes are used for seeing over crowds, observing wildlife from behind walls and in submarines for looking out over the surface of the sea.

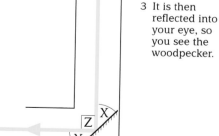

1 Light from the woodpecker hits the top mirror.

2 The light is reflected down to the bottom mirror.

3 It is then reflected into your eye, so you see the woodpecker.

7 What is a periscope made of?

8 What can a periscope be used for?

9 What are the angles between the light rays and the mirrors in a periscope?

 eye

10 Remote control devices for televisions don't use light. They use infrared radiation. Find out how a remote control works and in what ways infrared radiation is similar to light.

8K.4 Bending light

You can change the direction of a ray of light by bouncing it off a mirror. You can also change its direction by shining it into a different transparent substance. When you shine a ray of light from one substance into another it bends. These diagrams show what happens when you shine light into a thick block of glass or a bowl of water at different angles. The dotted line drawn on the diagrams is the normal.

When light bends like this the effect is called **refraction** (refraction means bending). We say that the light has been <u>refracted</u>. When there is a large angle between the light ray and the normal, the refraction (the bending) is quite large. When a light ray travels along the normal there is no refraction.

1 What does the word <u>refraction</u> mean?
2 How does the light have to enter the glass to produce a large amount of bending?
3 How does the light have to enter the glass for no refraction to happen?

Bending the light away from the normal

Refraction works in both directions. If you shine a ray of light out of a transparent substance like water or glass into air, it bends away from the normal. The only exception to this is if you shine it along the normal, when it doesn't bend at all.

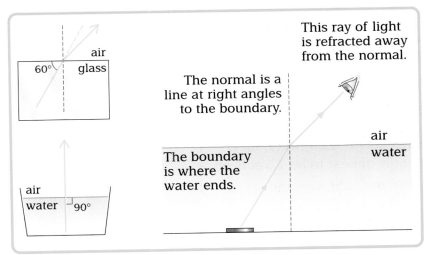

This ray of light is refracted away from the normal.

The normal is a line at right angles to the boundary.

The boundary is where the water ends.

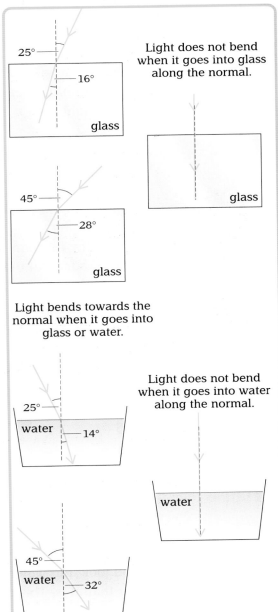

Light does not bend when it goes into glass along the normal.

Light bends towards the normal when it goes into glass or water.

Light does not bend when it goes into water along the normal.

You can use this effect to see round corners. In the top diagram Kris cannot see the coin because the light ray that travels past the edge of the metal can does not enter his eye. In the second diagram his friend Sam has added some water while Kris keeps his head still. The coin comes into view because the light ray from it is refracted (bent) as it comes out of the water. Kris can see the coin now because the light from it enters his eye.

4 How can you bend light away from the normal?
5 How must light travel out of a substance if it is not going to be refracted?

6 Explain why Kris can see the coin when the water has been added to the metal can.

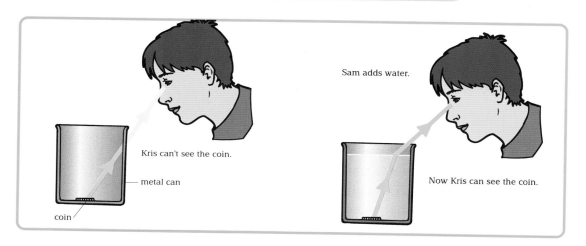

Kris can't see the coin.

metal can

coin

Sam adds water.

Now Kris can see the coin.

Water looks shallower than it is

When you look into water, refraction makes it look shallower than it is. This diagram shows what happens. The image of the fish does not appear to be as deep as the fish actually is.

This effect can be dangerous for people who cannot swim and who do not know that water seems shallower than it really is. A 2 m deep pool will only appear to be 1.5 m deep because of the refraction effect.

We can work out how deep an object is in water by multiplying how deep it appears to be by $\frac{4}{3}$.

7 Why does water appear to be shallower than it really is?

The boy looks shorter in water because light is refracted as it goes from water to air.

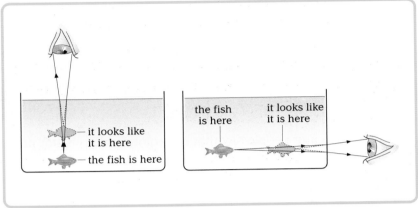

it looks like it is here

the fish is here

the fish is here · it looks like it is here

If you want to catch a goldfish by using a net, you will have to go deeper into the tank than you think if you look through the top surface. If you look through the side of the tank, the fish will appear at the correct depth but it will seem nearer! The refraction is always there to fool you when you look into water!

8 If a goldfish appears to be 15 cm deep in a fish tank, how deep is it really?

9 Find out what the critical angle is and what happens to light at the critical angle.

8K.5 The spectrum

If you go to Woolsthorpe Manor in Lincolnshire you can see a small room with a piece of glass set up to catch the Sun's rays coming through a hole in a window shutter. On the wall behind the glass the light forms a rainbow of colours. This is the room where Isaac Newton first did this experiment to show that white light is made up of colours, on 21 August 1665.

An easy way to show this is to shine white light through a specially shaped piece of glass or transparent plastic called a **prism**. The shape of the prism refracts the light twice in the same direction. The diagram shows you what happens.

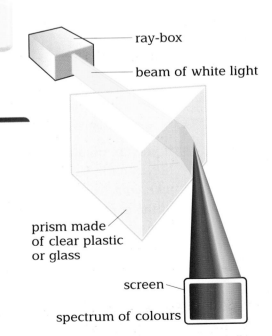

ray-box

beam of white light

prism made of clear plastic or glass

screen

spectrum of colours

The rainbow of colours is called a **spectrum**. If you look at a spectrum you will see that the colours gradually blend from one to the other, from a deep red at one end to a deep violet at the other. Many people remember the order of the colours using the phrase 'Richard Of York Gave Battle In Vain'. Each capital letter stands for a colour.

Some people say that the colour indigo is not present in the spectrum and that Newton invented it so he had seven colours rather than six. People thought that seven was a mystical number. It is a nice story but it does not make any difference. What actually matters is what is there to be seen. The seven-colour phrase is just a way of remembering the order. There are not actually any separate bands of colour in a spectrum, just a gradual change of shade.

1   What colours make up white light?
2   What is the name of the glass or plastic shape used to produce a spectrum?

3   Make up another phrase for remembering the order of colours in the spectrum.

Rainbows

Sometimes we see rainbows when the Sun is shining and it is raining at the same time. Obviously, showers of rain are not made of small prisms, but the raindrops work in a similar way.

If you are going to see a rainbow the angles have to be correct between the Sun, the rain and your eyes. You need to stand with your back to the sunlight. The angle between the direction of the sunlight and your line of sight to the raindrops must be about 42°. Red appears at the top of a rainbow and violet appears at the bottom.

4   Where does the Sun have to be for you to see a rainbow?
5   What is the order of colours in a rainbow, from the outside to the inside?

Drops of rain can split up sunlight into all the colours of the rainbow.

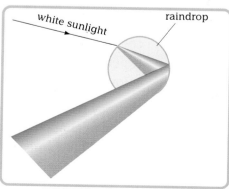

white sunlight   raindrop

You can make an artificial rainbow with a mist of drops from a garden hose.

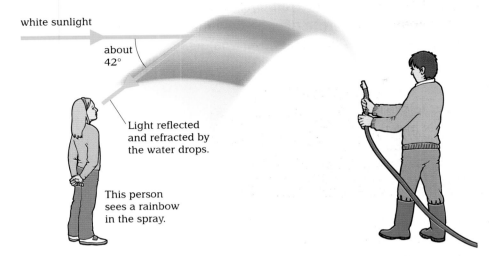

white sunlight

about 42°

Light reflected and refracted by the water drops.

This person sees a rainbow in the spray.

Another way of splitting white light into colours is to look at the reflection on the shiny side of a CD and tilt the CD at the same time. You can see some interesting rainbow patterns.

6 Give <u>two</u> different places where you might see a spectrum of colours that has not been produced by a prism.

7 Find out what colour blindness is.

8K.6 Colours

Coloured light can be made by passing white light through filters that only let some of the spectrum through. Coloured objects appear coloured because they only reflect certain parts of the white light spectrum.

Coloured filters

Coloured filters are sheets of plastic used to get coloured light from white light. They work by letting some of the spectrum through and absorbing other parts of it.

1 What colours does a red filter let through?

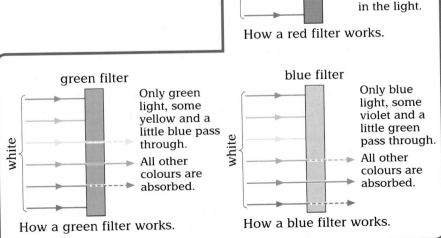

red filter

white

Only red light and a little orange pass through the filter.

The filter absorbs all other colours in the light.

How a red filter works.

green filter

white

Only green light, some yellow and a little blue pass through.

All other colours are absorbed.

How a green filter works.

blue filter

white

Only blue light, some violet and a little green pass through.

All other colours are absorbed.

How a blue filter works.

Red, green and blue are called the primary colours. There is an interesting effect that you can produce by using primary coloured filters. Because one third of the spectrum comes through the red filter, the middle third comes through the green filter and the final third comes through the blue filter, where they cross over you get white. You also get other colours where just two of the lights cross over.

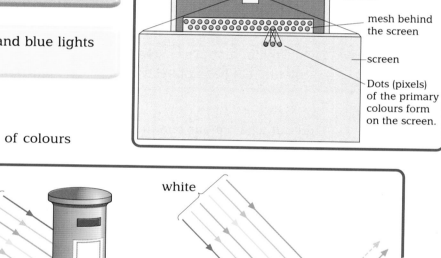

This idea is used in a colour television set. It generates three pictures on the screen: one is in red dots: one is in green dots and one is in blue dots. Because the dots are very close together, when you look at the screen you see the full range of colours depending on how bright the different dots are.

2 How many different colours of picture does a colour television have to produce for you to see the full range of colours?

3 Why does mixing red, green and blue lights produce white light?

Why things look coloured

White light is made up of a range of colours mixed together.

Red paint reflects red light and a little orange. It absorbs other colours.

Why grass looks green.

4 What colours from the spectrum does a red postbox absorb?

5 What colours from the spectrum does grass reflect?

6 Which parts of the spectrum do you think a yellow daffodil absorbs?

As well as getting different coloured objects by reflecting parts of the spectrum, you can get objects that are shades of grey, somewhere between white and black. These diagrams show how you get white, black and grey objects.

Things look different in different light

A postbox is red because it reflects red light and absorbs other colours. If you only have a green light and you shine it on a red postbox, the postbox will look black because there is no red light for it to reflect. Green grass will look green in the green light, but it will appear black if you shine red light on it because it absorbs red.

This effect can be a problem when you are buying coloured clothes or wallpaper or paint. The lighting in a shop is usually from a fluorescent tube and the balance of colours is different from the colours in sunlight. The bar charts show the difference between some common types of bulb and the Sun.

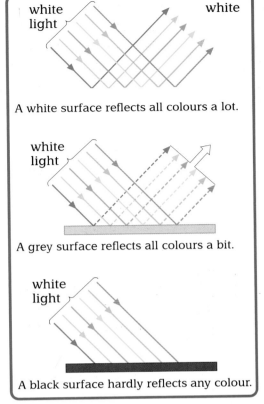

A white surface reflects all colours a lot.

A grey surface reflects all colours a bit.

A black surface hardly reflects any colour.

 7 Why might a red shirt look a different shade of red when you take it outside a shop?

 8 What colour would you expect blue jeans to look under the orange light of a street lamp? Give a reason for your answer.

 9 Find out what a daylight filter is and why it is sometimes used on a camera.

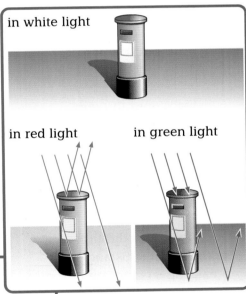

in white light

in red light

in green light

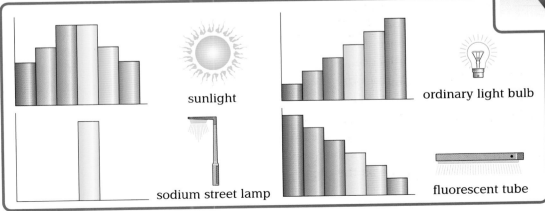

sunlight

ordinary light bulb

sodium street lamp

fluorescent tube

8K

You should now understand the key words and key ideas shown below.

Red filters let through red light and absorb the rest of the spectrum. Other colour filters work in a similar way.

A red **object** reflects red light and absorbs other colours so it will look black in pure green light. A blue object will appear black in pure red light because it absorbs red light and reflects blue light.

Light is represented by **rays**, which are straight lines with an arrow to show the direction the light travels in.

White light can be split into a **spectrum** by a **prism**. The colours are red, orange, yellow, green, blue, indigo and violet.

Light bends when it passes from one transparent substance to another. This is called **refraction**.

Light travels in straight lines at very high speed.

Light comes from **sources** like the Sun, flames, light bulbs and hot objects. These objects are **luminous**.

Light **reflects** off some objects so we see them. These object are **non-luminous**

Light goes through **transparent** things so you can see things through them. When light goes through we say it is **transmitted**.

Light

Light is **absorbed** by objects which appear black.

Light goes through **translucent** substances but breaks up so you cannot see things clearly through them.

Light reflects off a plane mirror so that the angle of incidence equals the angle of reflection. Angles are measured from the **normal**.

The **image** in a flat mirror appears as far behind the mirror as the **object** is in front of it.

Light is stopped by **opaque** substances which cast shadows.

The image in a flat mirror is the same size as the object.

The image in a flat mirror is the same way up as the object.

Sound and hearing

In this unit we shall learn about different types of sound and how they are made. We shall also learn about how we hear sound and how loud sounds can damage our hearing.

KEY WORDS
vibration
loudness
amplitude
pitch
frequency
hertz
oscilloscope
vacuum
decibel
noise pollution

8L.1 Making sound

Sound energy is a form of energy. It is made by things when vibrations are transformed into sound energy.

A **vibration** is a fast, backwards and forwards movement that repeats many times. Objects always vibrate to either side of their normal position. Try putting your fingers against your throat as you speak. You can feel your voice box vibrating. The kinetic energy of the vibrations is being changed into sound energy.

A loudspeaker makes sound when its paper cone vibrates backwards and forwards. This makes the air particles next to it vibrate. These vibrations are passed onto other air particles, rather like a Mexican wave. When the vibrations reach our ears, we hear the sound.

Vibrations can travel through different materials. Whales communicate by sending sound vibrations through the water. Earthquakes make vibrations in the ground that can be detected on the other side of the Earth.

You can hear the washing machine because it is vibrating.

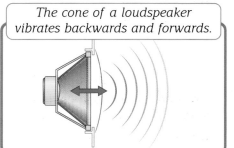

The cone of a loudspeaker vibrates backwards and forwards.

1   Look at the <u>two</u> diagrams of musical instruments. For each instrument, write down what is vibrating.

2   Name <u>three</u> materials that vibrations can travel through.

3   Explain how the sound of a drum reaches your ear. Use the word <u>vibrations</u> in your answer.

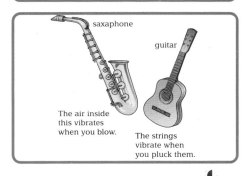

saxaphone

guitar

The air inside this vibrates when you blow.

The strings vibrate when you pluck them.

Making different sounds

Sounds can vary in **loudness**. Thunder is often a very loud sound but a whisper is a very quiet or soft sound. A loud sound has more energy than a quiet sound.

Yasmin can make a loud sound on the drum by hitting it very hard. This makes the drum skin move a long way from side to side and makes big vibrations of the air particles. We say that the vibrations have large **amplitude**. If Yasmin makes a quiet sound on the drum, the vibrations of the air particles are much smaller. The sound is quiet because the vibrations have small amplitude.

4 Write down an example of a loud sound.

5 How can Yasmin make a quiet sound on the drum?

6 Choose a different musical instrument. Describe how to make a loud sound and a quiet sound using this instrument.

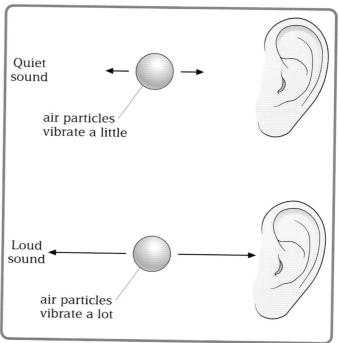

Quiet sound — air particles vibrate a little

Loud sound — air particles vibrate a lot

Sounds can also vary in **pitch**. A squeaky door produces a high-pitched sound and a big drum makes a low-pitched sound. Sometimes we can link the pitch of the sound to the size of the object that makes it. Big objects usually make low-pitched sounds because they vibrate slowly. Small objects make high-pitched sounds because they vibrate quickly.

7 Name <u>one</u> low-pitched sound and <u>one</u> high-pitched sound.

8 Look at the picture. Which instrument makes sounds of a lower pitch, the violin or the cello? Give a reason for your answer.

9 Why do you think a mouse makes a higher-pitched sound than a lion?

10 A male frog makes a low-pitched croaking sound when it is trying to attract a female frog in the spring. Find out how it makes such a low sound for its size.

Stuart's guitar has six strings of different thickness and 22 frets along its neck. If he plucks the thickest string, it produces a low-pitched sound. The thick string is heavy and so it vibrates slowly. We say that the string is vibrating at low **frequency**. The frequency is the number of vibrations in one second. It is measured in units called **hertz** (symbol Hz). The lowest note on the guitar only makes about 82 vibrations in one second, so its frequency is 82 Hz.

To make a high-pitched note he can pluck a thinner string. This vibrates faster because it is lighter. It makes a lot of vibrations in one second and we call this vibration a high frequency. The thinnest string makes about 330 vibrations in one second, so its frequency is 330 Hz.

Stuart can change the pitch and frequency of a sound in two other ways. He can press the string down against one of the frets. This makes the vibrating section of the string shorter. The shorter string vibrates at a higher frequency and makes a sound of higher pitch.

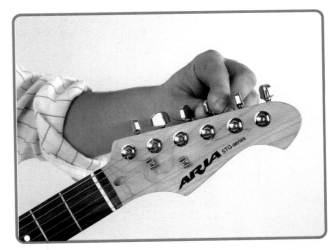

In Unit 7K we saw that the top E string on a guitar needs a force of about 75 N to make a note of the right pitch. Stuart turns the key to increase the force stretching the wire. This makes the string tighter so that the vibrations pass along its particles more quickly. Now the string vibrates at a higher frequency and produces a note of higher pitch.

11 What kind of vibration makes a high-pitched sound?
12 Describe <u>three</u> ways of making a higher pitched note on a guitar.
13 What is the frequency of the thinnest string on a guitar?

14 An oboe player plays the note A to help the orchestra tune up. This note has a frequency of 440 Hz. How many vibrations are there in one second?

Seeing sound waves

We cannot really see sound waves, but we can make a picture that represents them, using a microphone and an **oscilloscope**. The microphone changes the sound energy into tiny electric voltages which make the line on the oscilloscope move up and down.

The picture of a loud sound shows a tall wave. This is because the vibrations have large amplitude.

The picture of a quiet sound is smaller as the vibrations have small amplitude. The amplitude is shown on the oscilloscope as the height of the wave from the middle line to the crest, or top, of the wave.

The picture of a high-pitched sound shows the waves close together. This is because there are lots of vibrations in one second and the sound is of high frequency. The picture of a low-pitched sound shows the waves spread out. This is because there are fewer vibrations in one second and the sound is of low frequency.

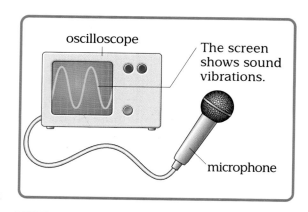

oscilloscope

The screen shows sound vibrations.

microphone

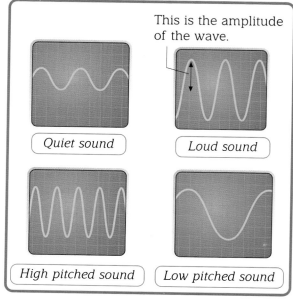

This is the amplitude of the wave.

Quiet sound

Loud sound

High pitched sound

Low pitched sound

15 Does a loud sound or a quiet sound produce the taller wave?

16 Which instrument, the flute or the piccolo, would produce the sound shown by:

 a oscilloscope A; **b** oscilloscope B?

17 The sound of Yasmin's voice looks like this on the oscilloscope. Explain why the wave is a complicated shape.

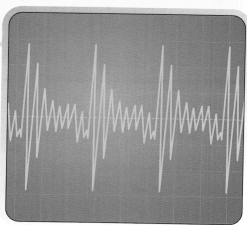

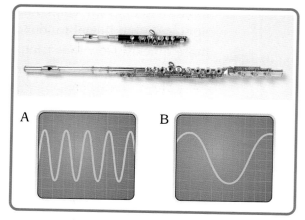

A

B

8L.2 Travelling sound

Sound travels as a series of vibrations through a material. Look at the diagram of a loudspeaker. The cone of the loudspeaker vibrates backwards and forwards. This pushes some air particles backwards and forwards. These push the next air particles, and so on, to make a sound wave.

We can see this happening if we put a candle flame in front of the loudspeaker. The flame vibrates backwards and forwards at the same frequency as the loudspeaker cone.

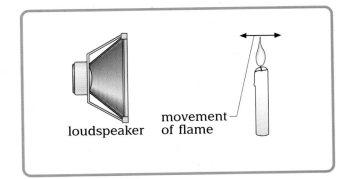

loudspeaker   movement of flame

Sound in a vacuum

In 1705, Francis Hauksbee showed a famous experiment, first performed by Robert Boyle in 1660, to an amazed audience in London. He put a bell inside a jar and made it ring. He used a pump to remove all the air from the jar to make a **vacuum**. A vacuum is an empty space that contains no particles at all. The audience could see the bell ringing but they could not hear it! Sound cannot travel through a vacuum because there are no particles to vibrate and carry the sound wave.

glass   air   vacuum

No sound can be heard.

1   What is a vacuum?

2   Hauksbee's audience could still see the bell vibrating. What does this tell us about light?

3   The Sun is an exploding ball of hot gases with a surface temperature of 5500 °C. Space is a vacuum. Why can we see the Sun but not hear the sound it makes?

4   Astronauts sometimes leave their spacecraft to mend a faulty satellite. Why do they use a radio system to talk to each other?

The speed of sound

In air, sound travels at a speed of about 330 metres every second. That is very fast – over 30 times faster than the world's fastest athlete!

The table shows that sound travels faster in water than in air. It travels even faster in solids like brick and iron. In *Spectrum Chemistry* Unit 7G we learnt that the particles in solids and liquids are closer together than those in a gas. The vibrations pass from particle to particle more quickly, so the wave travels faster.

Material	Speed of sound in m/s
air	330
water	1500
brick	3000
iron	5000

5   Draw a bar chart to show the speed of sound in different materials.

6   When a train is approaching a station we can usually hear the railway lines making a humming sound. Explain why we can hear this before we hear the train itself.

7   A whale sends a message to her mate 150 000 metres away. How long will the message take to reach him?

During a thunderstorm we see the lightning much earlier than we hear the thunder. Sound travels fast but light travels nearly a million times faster, at an amazing 300 million metres every second! Light could travel more than seven times round the Earth in one second!

8   How much faster does light travel than sound?

9   Describe <u>two</u> more examples which show that light travels much faster than sound.

10 If you marked the speed of light on your bar chart from question 5, how long would the bar be?

11 Describe how you could measure the speed of sound in air and in water. How would you make sure your value was accurate?

8L.3 Hearing sound

Look at the pictures of animals. They all have two ears but they can hear very different sounds.

A blackbird can hear very quiet sounds. It runs up and down on the grass to make worms think that it is raining. Then it listens for the sound of a worm moving in the ground so that it knows where to dig.

A dog can hear very high-pitched sounds. Dog owners sometimes blow on a special high-pitched whistle to call their dog even though they might not be able to hear the sound themselves.

A bat hears even higher sounds made by the insects that it eats. It can make very high-pitched sounds to find its way around in the dark. It listens for the echoes that are made when the sounds reflect off walls and other objects. This is called <u>echolocation</u>.

The bar chart shows the range of frequencies that different animals can hear. People can only hear sounds between 20 Hz and 20 000 Hz. This is a very small range compared with most animals. This range usually gets smaller as people get older. Your teacher will probably not hear the high-pitched notes as well as you do. Some people can hear fewer sounds, either because their hearing has been damaged by loud sounds or because of other causes.

1 Write a list of animals in order of the highest frequency they can hear.

2 As people grow older, which types of sound do they find it difficult to hear?

3 Make a list of sounds that an older person might not be able to hear. Test them out if you can.

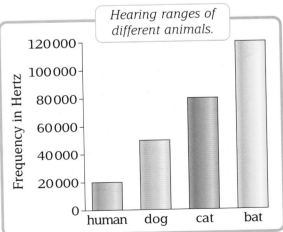

Hearing ranges of different animals.

The ear

Your ear is a very sensitive part of your body.

- A sound wave travels down the canal and makes the eardrum vibrate.
- These vibrations are passed onto the cochlea by a set of three small bones.
- In the cochlea, a liquid moves backwards and forwards and stimulates the nerve cells inside it.
- The nerve cells make small electrical signals.
- These electrical signals travel along the nerve to the brain.
- The brain receives an exact copy of the vibrations that made the sound wave.

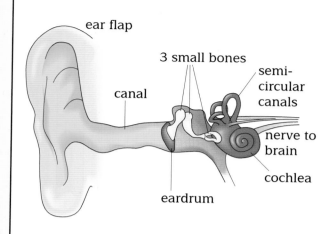

ear flap
3 small bones
semi-circular canals
canal
nerve to brain
cochlea
eardrum

4 What are the sound vibrations changed to before they reach the brain?

5 Draw a flow diagram for the ear, to show how vibrations in a sound wave send messages to the brain.

All animals have two ears. It helps the animal to find out where the sound is coming from. The owl hears the sound of its prey in both ears but the sound waves take slightly longer to reach its right ear. The owl's brain works out how far away its prey is. Then the owl turns his head round to make another measurement. Now he can swoop down and catch his prey.

The long-eared bat has huge earflaps, which collect more sound vibrations in the air. It can hear very quiet sounds and so it only needs to make quiet sounds for echolocation. This means that its prey insects cannot hear it coming!

6 Why do animals have two ears?

7 Which type of bat can hear the quieter sounds, the pipistrelle or the long-eared bat?

8 Find out how a stethoscope helps doctors to hear what is going on inside a patient.

long-eared bat

pipstrelle bat

8L.4 Dangerous sound

Loud sounds are made up of large vibrations, so the sound waves can carry a lot of energy. Very loud sounds can damage the ear and sometimes they cause pain. The loudness of a sound can be measured using a sound level meter. It is measured in units called **decibels**. The symbol for this unit is dB.

1 Which loudness level can permanently damage the ear? Give your answer in dB.

2 How loud is your classroom at the moment? Use the chart to judge the value.

3 People describe some sounds as noise. What do you think they mean by noise?

Making sound quieter

can cause hearing damage

The easiest way to make a sound quieter is to move away from the source – or to turn it down!

It is not always possible to do this, so other methods are used.

Cars have an exhaust pipe fitted to the engine and this has a silencer on it. This does not get rid of all the sound of the engine but it does make it a lot quieter. A car makes a very loud sound if it has a hole in its exhaust pipe!

At home, a room sounds very different when the curtains and carpets are taken out. This is because soft materials absorb sound vibrations and stop the sound from reflecting to make an echo.

An anechoic chamber is designed to absorb all sound. It is used for making very accurate measurements and recordings of sound.

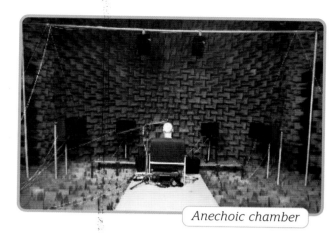
Anechoic chamber

The Royal Albert Hall in London has some strange mushroom-shaped saucers that hang from the ceiling to stop echoes. Recording studios and concert halls often have double glazing, or even triple glazing, installed to stop traffic noise from outside disturbing the performances.

Symphony Hall in Birmingham was built in 1991 and experts say that it has very good acoustics. This means that there is not very much unwanted sound and it is easy to hear the performers clearly.

There are strict laws that limit the noise level near places where people live and work. Too much noise is called **noise pollution**.

People working near loud machines wear earplugs or ear defenders. These absorb some of the sound vibrations.

Concorde can fly three times faster than sound. It is not allowed to fly faster than the speed of sound while it is over land. This is because it makes a very loud sound called a sonic boom.

4 What is meant by noise pollution?
5 Describe how to reduce echoes and traffic noise in a concert hall.
6 Why do people sometimes wear ear defenders at work?

7 Soft materials absorb sound vibrations. What happens to the energy of the sound waves?

Damaged hearing

Evelyn Glennie is a famous percussion player. She plays with different orchestras in concert halls all over the world. This is amazing as she became profoundly deaf when she was 12 years old. She says that she can feel the vibrations of the music through her body. In conversation, she speaks clearly and works out what other people are saying by watching their lips move. This is called <u>lip reading</u>.

People with very poor hearing are said to be deaf. You might be surprised to know that most deaf people can still hear some sounds.

There are many reasons why people have hearing problems. Some people are born with poor hearing. Others find that their hearing becomes worse after an illness or ear infection.

If the canal is blocked by earwax the vibrations cannot reach the eardrum. It is dangerous to clean out the earwax using a stick or cotton bud as this might damage the ear drum. The ear drum is a very thin layer of skin and muscle and so it breaks easily.

If the nerve cells in the cochlea are damaged, they do not send clear electrical signals to the brain. This is the most common cause of hearing problems in older people. Loud sounds can also damage the nerve cells in the cochlea. If you go to a loud pop concert or disco, you might become deaf for a few days. Sometimes the loud sounds cause a very annoying ringing sound in the ears called tinnitus. Both of these effects should go away after a few days. If you listen to very loud sounds for a long time, it can damage your hearing permanently.

 8 What most frequently causes older people to have hearing problems?

 9 Describe <u>one</u> way of breaking the ear drum.

 10 Evelyn Glennie is profoundly deaf. Find out what she can hear.

11 Find out more about the life of Evelyn Glennie by searching on the Internet.

12 Deaf people often use a sign language with their hands. Find out how to say a simple phrase using this sign language.

You should now understand the key words and key ideas shown below.

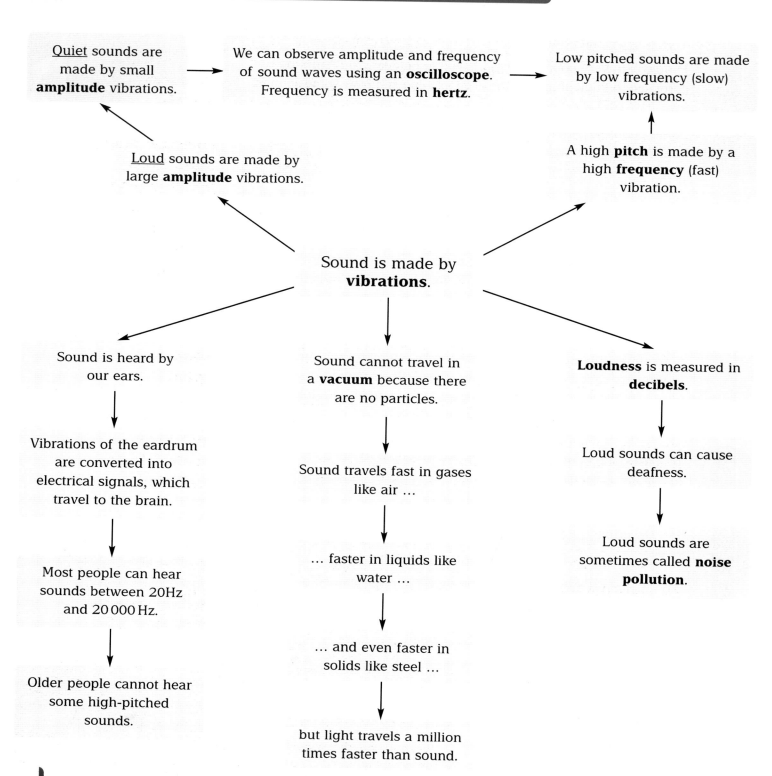

Quiet sounds are made by small **amplitude** vibrations.

We can observe amplitude and frequency of sound waves using an **oscilloscope**. Frequency is measured in **hertz**.

Low pitched sounds are made by low frequency (slow) vibrations.

Loud sounds are made by large **amplitude** vibrations.

A high **pitch** is made by a high **frequency** (fast) vibration.

Sound is made by **vibrations**.

Sound is heard by our ears.

Sound cannot travel in a **vacuum** because there are no particles.

Loudness is measured in **decibels**.

Vibrations of the eardrum are converted into electrical signals, which travel to the brain.

Sound travels fast in gases like air …

Loud sounds can cause deafness.

Most people can hear sounds between 20 Hz and 20 000 Hz.

… faster in liquids like water …

Loud sounds are sometimes called **noise pollution**.

Older people cannot hear some high-pitched sounds.

… and even faster in solids like steel …

but light travels a million times faster than sound.

Energy and electricity

In this unit, we shall study different energy transfers, and in particular the way electricity is used to transfer energy to do useful things. We shall investigate voltage and energy transfers round a circuit. We will also study how electricity is generated, and how this can affect the environment.

KEY WORDS
transform
transfer
device
chemical energy
fossil fuels
potential energy
kinetic energy
thermal energy
appliances
components
ammeter
voltage
potential difference
voltmeter
pylon
substation
National Grid
generator
nuclear fuels
radiation energy

91.1 How is energy involved in doing useful things?

In Unit 7I you learnt about different forms of energy. Whenever anything useful happens, one type of energy is changed (**transformed**) into another type of energy. A radio transforms electrical energy into sound energy, and **transfers** it to the surroundings.

Anything that changes energy from one form into another is called a **device**. We can group devices by the energy they use, for example devices that use electrical energy include toasters, DVD players and hairdryers even though they all give out different forms of energy. Other devices are grouped by the energy that they give out, for example heaters give out thermal energy. However, heaters use different forms of energy, for example electrical, or chemical energy, which is stored in coal, gas or oil.

1 How can devices be grouped?
2 Name <u>two</u> devices mentioned in the text.

3 Look at the photograph and write down <u>three</u> things that need electrical energy to work.

When we say that something 'uses electricity', we mean that electrical energy is changed into other useful forms of energy. Try to talk about electrical energy instead of electricity!

Some forms of energy can be stored for later use. Candles store **chemical energy** in their wax. During a power cut, a lit candle transforms this chemical energy into light and **thermal** (heat) **energy**. Chemical energy is also stored in **fossil fuels** such as oil, coal and gas, in food and in batteries.

Another way of storing energy is to give an object **potential energy** by changing its shape or by lifting it up. Springs in clockwork toys, a blown-up balloon or a stretched elastic band all store potential energy because their shape has been changed. This is called elastic potential energy. A skateboarder at the top of a ramp, and a person on a diving board have potential energy because of their positions. This is called gravitational potential energy.

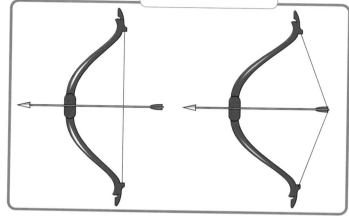

Stretching the bow stores elastic energy which is transferred to the arrow.

4 Write down <u>two</u> forms of energy that chemical energy can be turned into.

5 What has to change for an object to gain:

   a elastic potential energy;

   b gravitational energy?

6 Which of these examples have stored potential energy:

   a water at the top of a waterslide;

   b a child at the bottom of a slide;

   c a peanut butter sandwich;

   d an aeroplane in the sky;

   e a stretched spring?

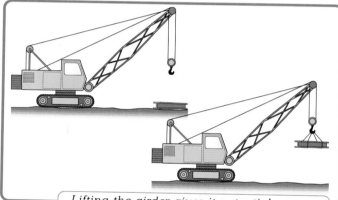

Lifting the girder gives it potential energy. If the girder falls, the gravitational potential energy is changed into kinetic energy.

Electrical energy cannot easily be stored but it is useful because it can be changed into so many other forms of energy. It is also a convenient and clean form of energy. Rechargeable batteries for mobile phones are charged up from the mains electricity supply, but the electrical energy changes into chemical energy before it is stored in the battery pack.

Chemical energy stored in the battery pack changes into electrical energy when the phone is used.

7 Which form of energy is stored in a battery pack?

8 Why are battery packs useful?

All electrical **appliances** include a circuit. As the electric current travels round the circuit in a radio, the loudspeakers transform electrical energy into sound energy. One way to describe energy transformations that take place in a device is like this:

type of energy put in ⟹ | device name | ⟹ type of energy coming out

For example:
electrical energy ⟹ | radio | ⟹ sound energy.

9 For each of the following, suggest a device that can carry out the energy transformation.

a electrical energy ⟹ [ ] ⟹ thermal energy

b electrical energy ⟹ [ ] ⟹ sound energy

c electrical energy ⟹ [ ] ⟹ light energy

d electrical energy ⟹ [ ] ⟹ kinetic energy

9I.2 How does electricity transfer energy?

The different parts of a circuit, such as bulbs, motors, loudspeakers and heaters, are called **components**.

As a current carries electrical energy round a circuit in a radio, it passes through the loudspeakers, which change this energy into sound. The current is not used up but returns to the battery to collect more electrical energy ready for its next trip round the circuit. When more current flows in the radio, more energy is carried from the battery. The sound from the loudspeakers becomes louder. An **ammeter** placed in the radio circuit will measure the size of the current flowing through that part of the circuit.

laboratory bulbs

domestic lightbulb

laboratory speaker

Hi-fi speaker

laboratory motor

washing machine motor

1 List <u>four</u> types of component.

2 An ammeter is placed in a radio to measure the current flowing through the loudspeaker. How does its reading change as the sound from a radio gets louder?

Simple circuits can be built as a single loop, called a series circuit. An example is the circuit found in a torch. Other circuits, called parallel circuits, are built with more than one loop. These include the circuit lighting a car's headlamps. In the parallel circuit, the current will divide between the loops (called branches), joining up at the far end. The total current in the circuit equals the sum of the currents in each branch.

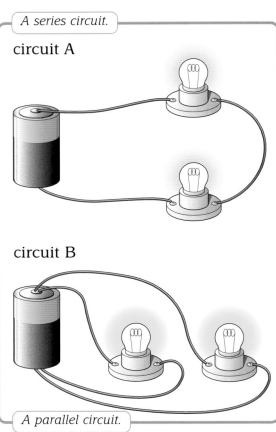

A series circuit.

circuit A

circuit B

A parallel circuit.

3   In a parallel circuit, the total current from the battery is 3 A. The ammeter in one branch of the circuit reads 2 A. What will the reading in the other branch to be?

Voltage makes the current flow round the circuit. A larger voltage forces more current to flow, carrying more energy. Batteries are labelled with their voltage. Car batteries normally have a voltage of 12.5 V because large currents are needed in the starter motor in the engine, but a watch uses a tiny current so its battery is only 1.3 V.

As the current passes through the circuit in the car, electrical energy is changed into **kinetic energy** and the voltage drops across the motor. Because there is a large energy change, the voltage drops a lot. Voltage is also called '**potential difference**'. A **voltmeter** is used to measure the difference in potential (voltage) on either side of components. In the car's engine, wires from the voltmeter are connected on each side of the motor, without breaking the circuit.

4   What happens when there is a larger voltage in a circuit?
5   Where is a voltmeter connected in a circuit?

A battery contains two (or more) cells joined together. The cells contain chemicals that react, producing a current when they are part of a complete circuit. The chemicals store chemical energy inside the battery. This chemical energy changes into electrical energy when the battery is part of a complete circuit.

6   What does the chemical energy in a battery change into in a circuit?

7 If a car battery loses 120 joules of chemical energy, how much electrical energy is transferred to the circuit?

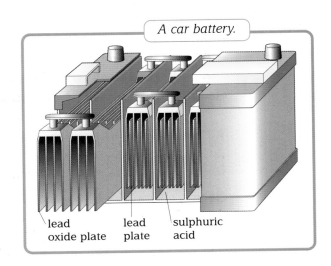

A car battery.

A car battery contains lead and lead oxide layers with sulphuric acid in between. Smaller batteries commonly used in household equipment are called dry cells. The liquid acid found in car batteries is replaced in dry cells with different substances like pastes, which are less likely to leak and damage equipment. So dry cells do not need to be kept level.

lead oxide plate · lead plate · sulphuric acid

8 Find out about the chemicals used in other types of battery.

Very high voltages are dangerous because of the large amounts of energy involved. When engineers work on high voltage transmission cables and **pylons**, or on electrified railway lines, the electricity travelling through the system must be switched off otherwise the engineers will be badly burned or killed. Sometimes, the voltages are so high that electricity can jump through the air to the nearest point connecting to earth. This happens in a thunderstorm when lightning strikes the highest point. This may be a tree or a tall building. In the same way, a person can get a fatal electric shock inside an electricity **substation**.

This tree was struck by lightning.

9 Why are high voltages dangerous?

10 A lightning conductor is a strip of metal on the side of a tall building. It is slightly higher than the roof and reaches the ground. How can the lightning conductor protect a building?

9I.3 Paying for and reducing the waste of electricity

Compare your home today with homes a hundred years ago. We now use many electrical appliances which can be plugged in and run from the mains supply. We use:

- lights instead of candles;
- electric cookers and electric heaters instead of open fires;
- TVs and music centres instead of playing family games;
- e-mails instead of writing letters.

Appliances such as fridges, washing machines and vacuum cleaners save many hours of housework. Each time you turn an appliance on, the electrical energy used is measured on your electricity meter and has to be paid for.

The reading from this electricity meter is used to prepare your electricity bill.

1 Write down <u>five</u> more appliances that use mains electricity.

Electric current from the mains supply carries electrical energy to components in each appliance where it changes into different forms of energy. The electrical energy is supplied at a high voltage (230 V in the UK), so a lot of energy can be supplied. Different appliances use up the energy at different rates. You will be pleased to hear that your CD player and TV use less energy per second than the vacuum cleaner, tumble dryer or cooker because they are less powerful. However, the longer the TV is left on for, the more energy is used up.

2 What voltage is mains electricity supplied at?

3 What <u>two</u> things affect how much energy an appliance uses?

It is possible to compare the energy used per second by examining a rating plate, which is found on most electrical items. The rating plate contains information about the voltage that the equipment works at, and its power. This is given in units of watts or kilowatts (a thousand watts). A watt is a measure of the amount of energy used by the appliance every second. It is measured in joules per second.

The power of the mobile phone charger is shown in watts (W) on the rating plate (circled in blue).

4 Write down the power rating of the mobile phone charger shown in the photograph.

5 Look at the table. List the equipment in order with the most powerful first.

Appliance	Typical energy used per second	Typical power
cooker	5000 joules	5 kilowatts
TV or computer	500 joules	500 watts
lamp	60 joules	60 watts
toaster	1200 joules	1.2 kilowatts

6 If a computer and lamp were each on for 3 hours, explain which one would add more to your electricity bill.

Some appliances transform nearly all the energy provided into forms of energy that we want. The percentage of energy transformed to the form we want is called the efficiency of the equipment.

Kettles are very efficient, and almost all the electrical energy provided is used to heat the water. Ordinary light bulbs are much less efficient. Only a small percentage of the electrical energy provided is changed into light, and the rest is turned into unwanted heat. Energy efficient light bulbs do not waste as much energy as heat, so more of the electrical energy changes into light.

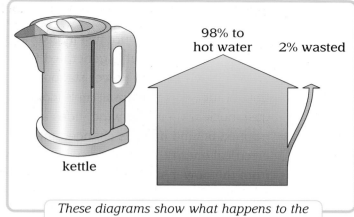

kettle

98% to hot water   2% wasted

These diagrams show what happens to the energy supplied to the appliance. The arrows show how much energy is turned into useful thermal energy, and how much is wasted.

 7 What does efficiency measure?

 8 Why do ordinary light bulbs use more electrical energy than energy efficient bulbs?

When energy is transferred, no energy is lost. However, it may not be in forms that we want, or be detected easily, or be reusable. All the energy transferred equals the original amount of energy provided. We say that the energy is conserved. Wasted energy is often unwanted sound or heat.

 9 Name <u>two</u> common forms of wasted energy.

 10 Write down the energy changes that take place in:

   a a light bulb;

   b a washing machine.

11 What forms of wasted energy are there when a light bulb and a washing machine are working?

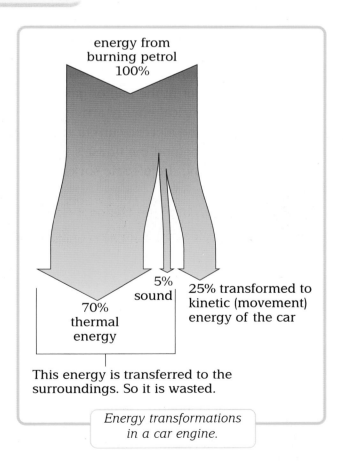

energy from burning petrol 100%

5% sound

25% transformed to kinetic (movement) energy of the car

70% thermal energy

This energy is transferred to the surroundings. So it is wasted.

Energy transformations in a car engine.

9I.4 Where do we get electrical energy from?

Mains electricity does not just appear at the socket in our walls but is generated first in a power station. In the power stations, energy from sources such as fossil fuels (coal, oil and gas), nuclear fuels, the wind, tides and water trapped behind dams is changed into electrical energy. An electric current flows from the power station, through the **National Grid**, to a substation and then to our homes.

The National Grid is a countrywide network of electric cables, supported by pylons, which links all power stations with substations. Substations are usually found in villages, and scattered through towns and cities. They change the very high voltages supplied by power stations into smaller, safer voltages for home use. Power cables in the street or buried underground carry the electrical energy from electricity substations to our homes. This way, our homes receive electrical energy safely from different power stations.

An electricity meter (often found under the stairs, or in the hall or garage) measures all electrical energy arriving at the house. Then the electric current travels through wires behind the house's walls before reaching the electric sockets.

Electricity pylons carry very high voltage electricity safely around the country.

Electricity substations contain transformers which alter the voltage.

1   What is the National Grid?
2   What does an electricity substation do?

3   Why do houses need electricity meters?

All that is needed to produce electrical energy is a magnet and a coil of wire forming part of a circuit. When either the magnet or the coil moves, a current flows in the circuit. This is because their kinetic energy is changed into electrical energy. The magnet and coil of wire are called a **generator** because they generate (create) an electrical current.

The current does not flow unless the coil or magnet is moving. This means that electrical energy cannot be stored. Instead, the energy is stored in the fuels and other energy sources that supply the power stations. If there is a surge in electricity demand, the power stations must supply more electrical energy quickly or there will be power cuts.

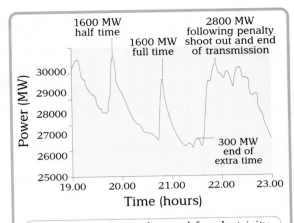

4 What does a generator do?

5 What energy change takes place in a generator?

The graph shows demand for electricity during the 1990 England–Germany World Cup semi-final. Surges in demand were caused by kettles and lights being turned on and water pumped when toilets were flushed.

There are many ways to make generators spin, even though they are massive and weigh several tonnes each. Most generators are connected to a turbine. A turbine has blades and spins when steam or air is blasted at it, just as a windmill's blades spin when it is windy. As the turbine spins, the generator spins too.

The steam is created by heating water in fossil fuel power stations and in nuclear power stations. The thermal energy needed is released when coal, oil or natural gas are burned, or when **nuclear fuels** split up into other substances and produce **radiation energy**.

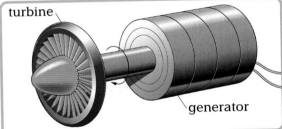

6 Why is a turbine used in power stations?

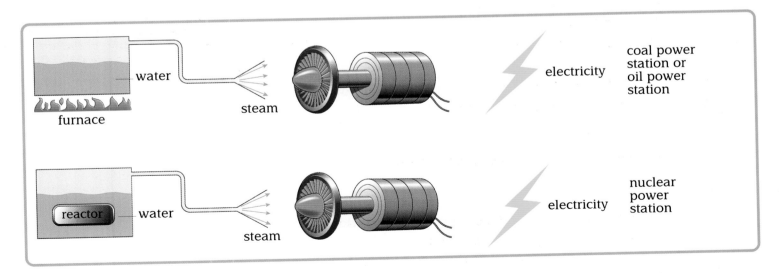

You should now understand the key words and key ideas shown below.

- Whenever anything happens, one type of energy is changed (**transformed**) into another type of energy or is **transferred** to a different place.

- Anything that changes energy from one form into another is called a **device**.

- **Chemical energy** is stored in fuels such as oil, coal and gas (**fossil fuels**), in food and in batteries.

- **Thermal energy** and light energy are released when candles are lit.

- **Potential energy** is stored when an object changes its shape or position.

- Electrical energy is useful because it can be changed into many other forms of energy and is convenient and clean.

- The different parts of a circuit are called **components**.

- A battery contains two (or more) cells joined together. The cells contain chemicals which react, producing a current when they are part of a complete circuit.

- **Voltage** or **potential difference** from a battery or the mains forces current to flow round a complete circuit.

- A larger voltage forces more current to flow. A **voltmeter** measures the size of the voltage.

- When more current flows, more energy is carried from the battery. An **ammeter** measures the size of the current flowing through it.

- If we add up all forms of energy transformed, it equals the original amount of energy provided.

- The electricity travels from a power station through the **National Grid** until it reaches an electricity **substation** where its voltage is lowered. Cables carry the electricity to houses, where it passes through an electricity meter before travelling through wires to electrical sockets and **appliances**.

- In a power station, a turbine spins a **generator** when steam or air is blasted at it, which generates electrical energy.

Pressure and moments

In this unit we shall look at the effects of forces acting in two different ways, pressure and moments.

KEY WORDS
force
pressure
area
compress
pneumatic
molecules
gas
compressible
balanced forces
incompressible
liquid
hydraulic
moment
pivot
lever
load
effort

9L.1 What is pressure?

When a **force** pushes on a surface, it produces an effect called **pressure**. You apply pressure to the ground through the sole of your shoe for example. Pressure is a measure of how concentrated a force is on the **area** of the surface.

Applying pressure

The pressure a force produces depends on two things:

- the size of the force;

- the area it acts on.

If you press on the grass with your hand flat, you do not disturb the soil. But if you use a pointed stick to press with the same force, the point digs into the ground. This is because the same force acting on a smaller area produces greater pressure.

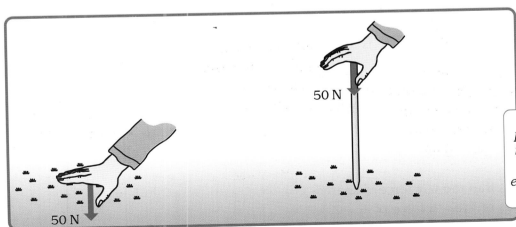

50 N

50 N

You can easily apply a 50 N push with your hand. This force is about the same as the weight of 5 kg bag of potatoes. The effect of a 50 N force depends on the area to which you apply it.

1   What <u>two</u> things does pressure depend on?

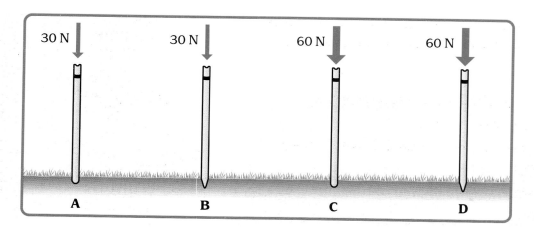

2 Look at the pictures.

a Which stump exerts the least pressure on the ground?

b Which stump exerts the greatest pressure on the ground?

c Which stump will be pushed furthest into the soil?

Using the pressure formula

If you know the force and the area, you can always calculate the pressure with the formula:

> pressure = force ÷ area

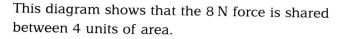

To use this formula correctly the area must be perpendicular (at right angles) to the force. For example, you can use this formula to find out which exerts a greater pressure, a force of 8 N on an area of 4 mm², or a force of 6 N on an area of 2 mm².

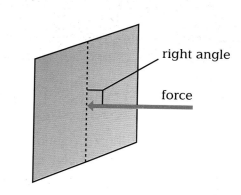

This diagram shows that the 8 N force is shared between 4 units of area.

A force of 8 ÷ 4 = 2 N acts on each square millimetre. We say that the pressure is 2 N per mm² (N/mm²).

> pressure = 8 N ÷ 4 mm² = 2 N/mm²

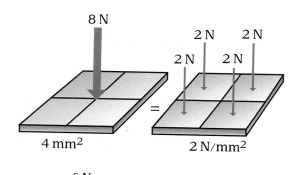

This diagram shows that the 6 N force is shared between just 2 units of area. A force of 6 ÷ 2 = 3 N acts on each square millimetre. We say that the pressure is 3 N per mm².

> pressure = 6 N ÷ 2 mm² = 3 N/mm²

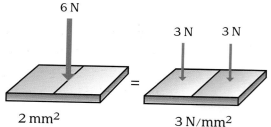

Even though the 6 N force is smaller than the 8 N force, it exerts a greater pressure. This is because it is concentrated on a smaller area.

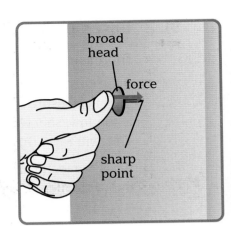
broad head
force
sharp point

3 a Where is the pressure greater, on the head of the drawing pin, or under the point?

b Explain why a drawing pin is designed with a sharp point and a broad head.

4 Explain why truck tyres sink into the mud, but tractor tyres do not.

5 Find the pressure for each of these combinations of force and area:

a force = 10 N, area = 5 mm²

b force = 20 N, area = 4 cm²

c force = 55 N, area = 0.1 m² 550pa

d force = 10 000 N, area = 2.5 m² 4000 pa

Pressure units

The unit of pressure is $1 N/m^2$. This unit is given the name the pascal (Pa).

$$1 N/m^2 = 1 Pa$$

Pressure points

Sitting on a broad bicycle saddle is more comfortable than sitting on a narrow racing saddle. The broad saddle supports your weight over a larger area. Because the supporting force is spread out more, it applies a smaller pressure.

6 Explain why shaped chair seats are more comfortable than flat, hard seats, using the idea of pressure.

A

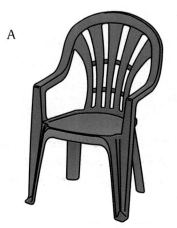

B

9L.2 Gases under pressure

Increasing pressure

A car driver uses a pressure gauge to check the air pressure in her tyres. If the pressure is too low, she pumps more air into the tyre. This will raise the pressure.

Air is a gas. It can be **compressed** (squeezed into a smaller volume) by applying pressure. A simple pump applies pressure through a moving piston. The piston compresses the air inside the cylinder. The increased pressure forces the air through the valve into the tyre.

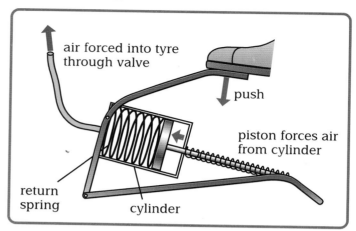

Machines that make use of gas pressure are described as **pneumatic**.

 1 What forces air into the tyre?

 2 The diagram shows pressure applied to a gas by a weighted piston. How will the piston move if half the weights are removed?

 3 What word describes machines that use gas pressure?

 4 Find out how an aerosol can, a water rocket, a peashooter and a steam engine use gas pressure to operate. In each case explain how the pressure is produced and how it is used.

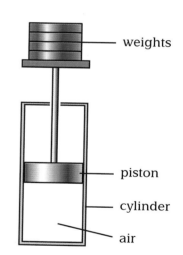

Moving molecules

The **molecules** in a **gas** are moving around at random in all directions and they will take up as much space as they have. So, a gas expands to fill its container. This means that gas molecules can be widely spaced apart, for example the average distance between air molecules in a room is about 10 times the size of a molecule.

There is plenty of empty space between the molecules. This means that molecules can be pushed closer together, and so a gas can be compressed into a smaller volume. We say it is **compressible**.

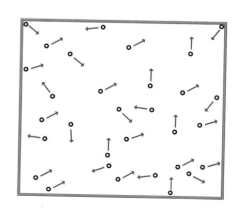

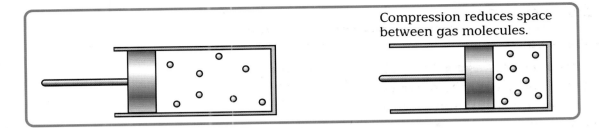
Compression reduces space between gas molecules.

5 Why can gases be compressed?

Newton's third law states:

For every force there is an equal force that acts in the opposite direction.

Pushing back

When you apply pressure to compress a gas, the gas pushes back with an equal and opposite pressure. This is an example of Newton's third law of motion. The pressure of the gas is created by the gas molecules as they collide with, and rebound from, the piston.

The gas molecules apply an equal pressure on all parts of the container walls. For example, the pressure of the gas inside an inflated beach toy keeps the wall stretched to give the toy its shape.

Gas pressure is increased when more molecules are added to the same volume. This is because more molecules collide with the container walls each second.

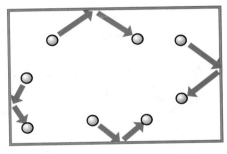
Molecules moving at random strike walls and rebound – applying pressure.

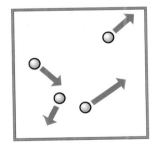 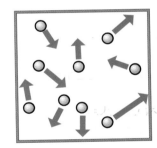

Gas pressure is also increased when a fixed amount of gas is compressed into a smaller volume. This is because the gas molecules are closer together, so on average they collide more frequently with each unit of area of the container walls.

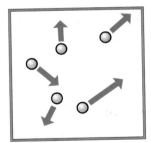

6 How do gas molecules apply pressure to the walls of their container?

7 Explain why pumping more air into an inflated football increases the pressure of the gas inside.

8 Explain why pressing down the plunger on a sealed syringe increases the pressure of the gas inside.

9L.3 Liquids under pressure

Incompressible water

A sealed plastic bottle filled with air and a second bottle filled with water feel very different if you squeeze them. The air-filled bottle squashes, but the water-filled bottle does not. Air compresses into a smaller volume when pressure is applied. Water is almost completely **incompressible**.

1 Which bottle is more difficult to squash? Explain why.

2 The forces applied to the pistons are increased.

   a Which piston moves?

   b Which piston does not move? Explain why.

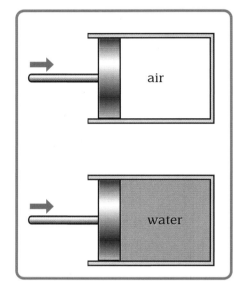

Crowded molecules

Unlike a gas, molecules in a **liquid** are crowded closely together. There is very little empty space between the molecules to close up when pressure is applied.

3 Which diagram shows the molecules:

   a in a gas;

   b in a liquid?

4 Which sample is:

   a compressible;

   b incompressible?

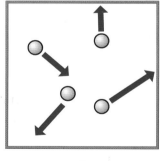

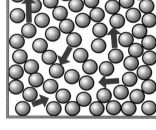

A   B

Under pressure

When pressure is applied to a liquid, the liquid pushes back with an equal and opposite pressure. The more pressure is applied, the more the pressure of the liquid rises. The pressure is the same at every point throughout the liquid. If it were not, liquid would move from high pressure to low pressure to even out the difference.

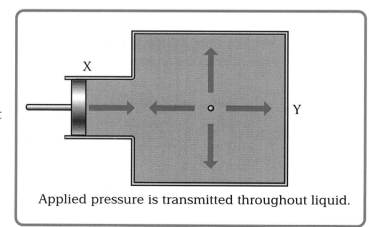

Applied pressure is transmitted throughout liquid.

5 A pressure of $10\,\text{N/cm}^2$ is applied at X. What is the pressure at Y?

Transmitting pressure

Water and other liquids can transmit pressure and forces from place to place. Look at the diagram. Yasmin applies a force to the plunger of syringe A. The force increases the pressure of the water in the syringe. The pressure is transmitted through the tube to syringe B by the water. To stop the plunger in syringe B from moving out, Eric must apply an equal but opposite pressure. Since the syringe plungers have the same area, the force required is the same.

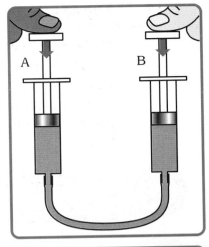

6   Yasmin applies a force of 5 N. The area of the plunger is 0.4 cm².

   a What is the pressure increase?

   b What force must Eric apply to balance this pressure?

Look at the picture. Aftab finds it difficult to stop plunger B moving because plunger B has a larger area. This means that a larger force is needed to produce the same pressure.

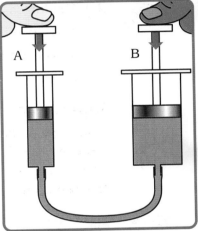

7   Which quantity, force or pressure, is the same throughout the liquid?

8   On which plunger, A or B, must the force be increased to produce the same pressure?

Hydraulics

Hydraulic systems use liquids to transmit forces. The hydraulic brakes in a car use hydraulic fluid (a type of oil) to transmit the pressure produced by the driver's foot on the brake pedal to the brake cylinders. Pistons in the brake cylinders push the brake pads.

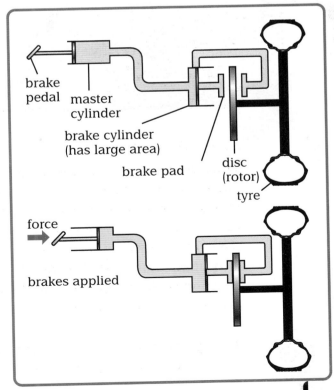

9   a Is the pressure in the brake cylinder different from the pressure in the master cylinder? If so, how?

   b How is the braking force produced by the brake cylinder different to the force applied by the driver's foot?

10 It is very dangerous if a slow leak allows air bubbles into the brake fluid. Explain why the brakes might not work properly.

Pressure and depth

If you dive under the water, you can feel the pressure on your ears increasing as you get deeper. At the surface the pressure is one atmosphere. The pressure under water is created by the weight of the water above pushing down. The pressure on a skin-diver 10 m down is 2 atmospheres, double the pressure at the surface.

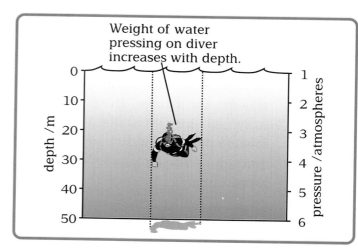
Weight of water pressing on diver increases with depth.

11 What is the pressure at a depth of 50 m?

12 Why is it dangerous for a submarine to dive below the maximum depth for which it is designed?

13 Explain how this demonstration shows that pressure changes with depth in a liquid.

9L.4 Turning forces

Making things turn

You need to push or pull to open this door. The door pivots on hinges at one side, so the force does not move the door in a straight line. The force makes the door turn. The turning effect of a force is called its **moment**.

turning effect of force

force

1 What do we call a turning effect caused by a force?

Clockwise and anticlockwise moments

The weight of the boy produces a clockwise turning force on the seesaw. The moment of the boy's weight turns the seesaw in the same direction as the hands on a clock. The weight of the girl turns the seesaw in the opposite direction. It produces an anticlockwise moment.

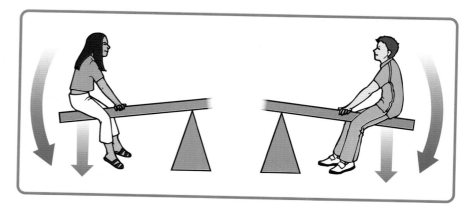

2 The diagrams show some more forces with moments around pivots. In each case, state which way the object will turn.

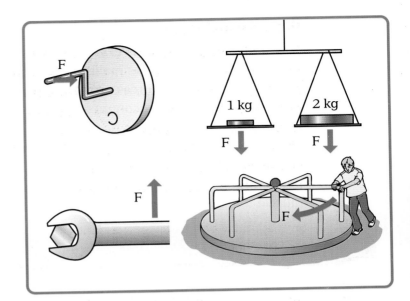

Changing the moment

The size of a turning moment depends on two things:

● the size of the force;

● its distance from the **pivot**.

It is easier to open a door if you push as far from the hinge as possible. The same force applied further from the hinge has a bigger moment.

3 What <u>two</u> things does the size of a moment depend on?

4 Which force, A, B or C, produces the greatest moment on the door?

A spanner provides a moment to undo a nut. If the nut is too tight, you can increase the turning effect of the force by using a longer spanner.

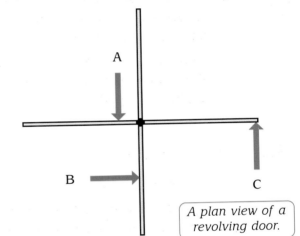

A plan view of a revolving door.

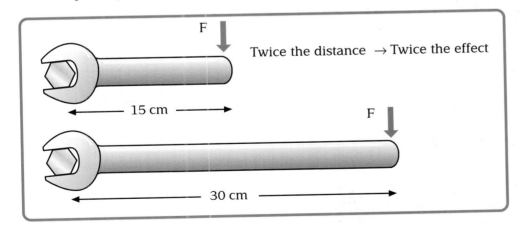

Twice the distance → Twice the effect

15 cm

30 cm

5 What are the <u>two</u> ways you can increase the turning effect of a spanner on a nut?

6 How can you make a moment smaller? Give <u>two</u> ways.

Body levers

Your arms and legs are **levers**. Your joints are pivot points. Your muscles make your limbs bend by producing turning forces around your joints. Muscles apply forces by contracting. They can only pull, not push. So you need a pair of muscles to operate your limbs at each joint. One muscle to bend, the other to straighten. The muscle that bends your arm at the elbow is the biceps. The muscle that straightens it again is the triceps.

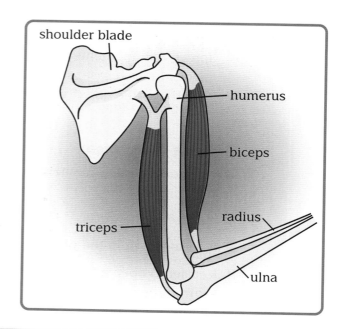

7 Name <u>two</u> parts of your body that act as:

a levers; **b** pivots.

Calculating moments

To use this formula correctly, the force must be at right angles to the line from the pivot to the place where the force acts.

You can work out a moment with this formula:

moment = force × distance of force from pivot

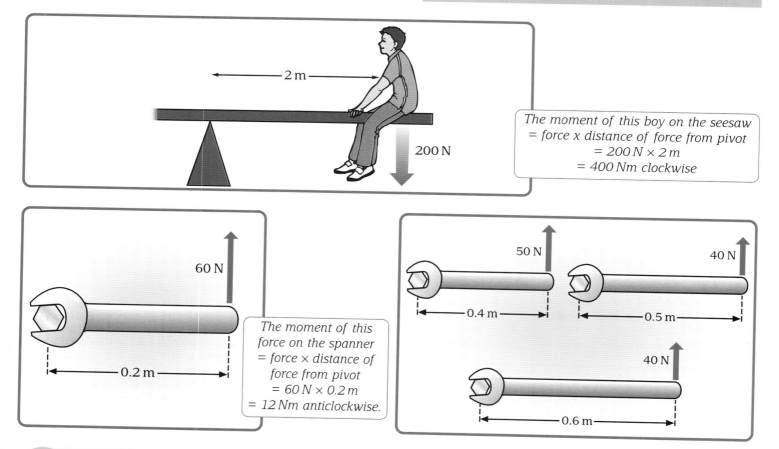

The moment of this boy on the seesaw
= force x distance of force from pivot
= 200 N × 2 m
= 400 Nm clockwise

The moment of this force on the spanner
= force × distance of force from pivot
= 60 N × 0.2 m
= 12 Nm anticlockwise.

8 Find the moments in each of these examples. Which spanner produces the biggest moment on the nut?

9L.5 Balance and levers

Balancing a seesaw

A smaller person can balance a larger person on a seesaw by sitting further from the pivot. We can use moments to explain how balance works.

The weight of the smaller person in the example produces an anticlockwise moment.

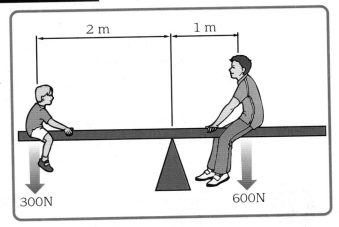

anticlockwise moment = weight A × distance A
= 300 N × 2 m
= 600 N m

The weight of the larger person produces a clockwise moment.

clockwise moment = weight B × distance B
= 600 N × 1 m
= 600 N m

To be in balance, the anticlockwise moment must equal the clockwise moment.

anticlockwise moment = clockwise moment
weight A × distance A = weight B × distance B
300 N × 2 m = 600 N × 1 m

From this formula we can see that because person A is just half the weight of person B, he must sit twice as far from the pivot to produce the same size moment.

This balance formula is called the principle of moments. The principle states that balance is achieved when:

anticlockwise moment = clockwise moment

1 What must happen for a seesaw to balance?

2 Where must you position the weight to balance the load on this beam balance?

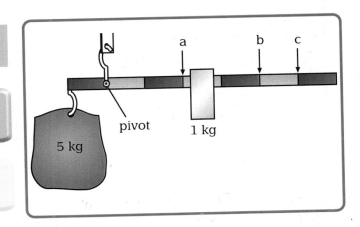

Balanced machines and bodies

A tower crane must be kept in balance when it lifts a **load**, or it will topple over. The load on this crane produces a clockwise moment about the top of the tower. This is balanced by a counterweight that produces an anticlockwise moment.

 3 What do cranes use to remain balanced when they lift loads?

 4 Which way must the counterweight be moved after the crane driver has released this load? What would happen if the counterweight were not shifted?

The weight can be shifted towards or away from the tower to maintain balance when the crane lifts different size loads.

As the gymnast leans forward, her upper body produces an anticlockwise moment about her foot (the balance point). She produces a balancing clockwise moment by extending her free leg in the opposite direction.

 5 Use moments to explain why the counterweights must be present when the truck lifts a load.

They may not realise it, but when dancers and gymnasts balance, they are using the principle of moments.

 6 How do gymnasts use the principle of moments to remain balanced?

Levers

A lever is a simple machine that uses moments to apply and change forces. This girl is applying a force (called an **effort**) at one end of the lever to lift a weight (called a load) on the other side of the pivot.

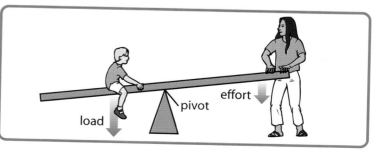

The principle of moments shows how the girl can use a small effort to lift a larger load. She must apply the effort further from the pivot than the load.

> principle of moments applied to a lever:
>
> effort × distance from effort to pivot = load × distance from load to pivot

A lever used in this way increases the effort. We say levers <u>magnify</u> effort. But you never get something for nothing! If the lever increases the force, then the distance moved is decreased. The girl pushes through a large distance to lift the toddler a small distance.

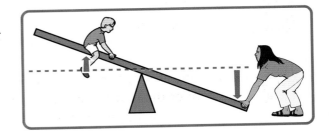

7 a What does a lever magnify?

b How does the lever do this?

8 Use a ruler to measure the effort to pivot and load to pivot distances on the nail extractor. Use your measurements and the principle of moments to calculate how many times it magnifies the effort.

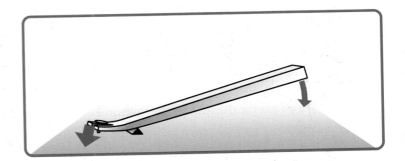

Magnifying distance

People also use levers to magnify distance. For example a long fishing rod converts a small movement of the hands to a large movement of the rod tip.

A rowing oar is another example of a lever used in this way.

9 Look at the picture of the rower.

a Identify the objects that are the effort, pivot and load in this diagram.

b Which force is greater, the effort or the load?

c Which moves further, the effort or the load?

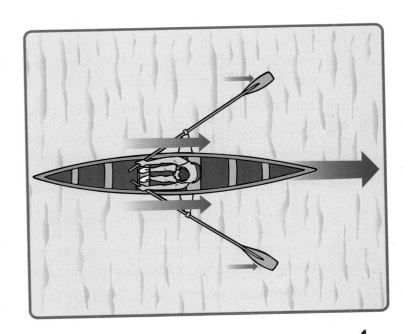

You should now understand the key words and key ideas shown below.

- **Pressure** is the effect of a **force** acting on an **area**. Pressure can be increased either by increasing the force or by decreasing the area.
- Pressure can be calculated from the formula:

  pressure = force ÷ area

- The SI unit of pressure is the newton per square metre (N/m^2). This unit is called the pascal (Pa).

  $1 \, N/m^2 = 1 \, Pa$

- **Gas** pressure is produced by gas **molecules** colliding with the container walls, and with anything in the gas.
- A gas is **compressible**. It can be squeezed into a smaller volume by increasing the pressure on it.
- **Pneumatic** describes the action of machines that use gas pressure to work.
- A **liquid** is **incompressible**, it cannot be squeezed into a smaller volume.
- Applied pressure is transmitted throughout a liquid or a gas inside a container.
- **Hydraulic** describes the action of machines that use liquid pressure to work.
- Pressure increases with depth. This is because the weight of the liquid or gas overhead increases with depth.
- The turning effect of a force is called its **moment**.
- The moment of a force can be increased either by increasing the force, or by increasing the distance of the force from the turning point (**pivot**).
- The moment of a force can be calculated from the formula:

  moment = force × distance of force from pivot

- The principle of moments states that an object is balanced when clockwise and anticlockwise turning moments are equal.
- A **lever** uses the principle of moments to amplify the force, or the distance moved, when an **effort** is used to move a **load**.

Scientific investigations

Throughout Key Stage 3 you will look at investigations carried out by scientists, past and present, and carry out your own investigations. This chapter will remind you of the skills you learnt at Key Stage 2 and will help you to practise and improve them. It will also introduce new skills.

Planning investigations

Finding suitable questions for investigations

When you do an investigation, you have a question to answer. Then you plan an investigation that you hope will give you the answer. But you can't answer all questions by doing a scientific investigation.

1 Look at parts **a** to **c**. Can you answer them by doing a scientific investigation? Explain your answers.

  a Is there a link between the height of a cat and the length of its whiskers?

  b Where is the rainiest place on Earth? (You can't visit everywhere on Earth, but lots of scientists have collected data about rainfall in lots of places.)

  c Are waterfalls beautiful? (Think about whether people agree on what is beautiful!)

Now think about the question of why elephants throw water over themselves. You can't answer it directly, but you can do an investigation using a model.

First, you need to think of ideas that might explain why elephants throw water over themselves. We call these ideas **hypotheses**.

Elephants often spray water over themselves like this.

hypotheses
prediction
sample size
sampling
random
surveys
secondary data
relevant
reliable
accurate
validity of results
preliminary tests
variable
vary
control
range
scale
precision
hazards
risk
risk assessment
mean
bar chart
line graph
data collection
presenting results
conclusion
evidence
evaluation
anomalous results
opinions
biased

The idea that elephants do this to cool themselves is one that you can test. You probably haven't got an elephant, so you have to use a model! A plastic bottle full of hot water makes a suitable model. You can use a thermometer or a temperature probe and a datalogger to show any temperature changes.

The elephants are:
* just having a wash;
* trying to cool themselves;
* getting rid of parasites;
* chasing away flies;
* just playing.

2   Draw your idea of what the model elephant apparatus looks like.

3   Remember that you are trying to find out if water makes the elephants cooler.

   a   Describe how to model throwing the water over the elephant.

   b   What measurements will you need to write down?

Next, you need to say what you think your results will be. This is called making a **prediction**. You need to use the science that you know to give reasons for your prediction. Kirsty has made a prediction:

I think that when we pour cold water over the plastic bottle, the temperature of the water inside will fall.

4   Do you think that Kirsty's prediction is correct? Explain your answer as fully as you can. Remember that an explanation using scientific ideas will get you the best marks.

Choosing the best strategy for an investigation

Often there are several possible ways of doing an investigation. However, one method may be better than the others. For example, one way may be easier, safer or produce more useful data than all the other methods.

You are likely to have done investigations involving fair testing in which you learnt about the importance of controlling variables. However, some variables are easier to control than others. Physical factors such as light and temperature are fairly easy to control.

Living things are a particular problem because they themselves vary. So when you investigate living things, you use 10 or 20 or more, not just one. We call this using a sample. You have to think about a suitable **sample size**. In *Spectrum Biology* Unit 8D you learn how to estimate the numbers of different living things by **sampling** using quadrats.

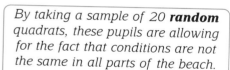

*By taking a sample of 20 **random** quadrats, these pupils are allowing for the fact that conditions are not the same in all parts of the beach.*

5   Explain why the sample needs to be random.

You can also use sampling to do **surveys** of data about people, including people's opinions. These often involve questionnaires.

Information collected by other people is useful in some investigations. We call the information **secondary data**. Examples are the data in leaflets produced by companies, consumer reports, libraries and the Internet. You need to be careful as some of this information may be biased.

You can find out information from secondary sources such as this.

6 List some secondary sources of information about factors affecting the pH of soil.

Collecting appropriate data

To answer your question, the data that you collect must be relevant, reliable and accurate. So you need to:

- choose a suitable design of your investigation to ensure that your evidence is **relevant**. That is why scientists often do trial runs. Relevant evidence is evidence that will help you to answer your question;

- record sufficient observations or readings to ensure that your evidence is **reliable**;

- choose suitable measuring instruments and take accurate and precise readings to ensure that your evidence is **accurate**.

The **validity of results** depends on the accuracy and precision of the <u>measuring instruments</u> that you choose and <u>how well you use them</u>.

Using preliminary work such as trial runs

Scientists often do trial runs of experiments to find out whether their approach will work or not.

Mrs Tasker asked her class to find out which of three varieties of apples gave the most juice by finding out how much of each apple is water. She set her class some preliminary work using books to research a method. No one found that actual experiment, but Bryan found one about the amount of water in soil. Using the same idea, he suggested an experiment:

- Find the mass of an apple.
- Heat it to get rid of all the water.
- Find its mass again. The loss in mass will be equal to the mass of water that was in the apple.

Anna found out that you needed to repeat this several times until two masses were the same. It is called heating to constant mass and you do it so you can be sure that all the water has gone. Lee thought that chopping the apple might make drying faster.
Mrs Tasker was pleased with the ideas so far – but she pointed out that they hadn't described how to heat the apple.

She suggested that they needed to do some **preliminary tests**. They needed to try out their ideas to find out which one worked best.

7 What <u>two</u> kinds of preliminary work did the class do before they planned their investigation?

	Heat over Bunsen flame		Dry on an open shelf at 20°C		Heat in an oven at 100°C		Heat in an oven at 300°C	
Size of apple pieces	cut into 1/8ths	chopped up small	cut into 1/8ths	chopped up small	cut into 1/8ths	chopped up small	cut into 1/8ths	chopped up small
Mass at start (g)	140.8	136.4	142.3	143.5	138.6	136.7	133.6	139.1
Mass after 40 mins (g)	12.7	10.1	137.6	135.2	103.5	100.8	10.9	10.1
Mass after 1 day (g)	not done	not done	69.1	67.7	17.3	16.2	9.4	8.4
Mass after 7 days (g)	not done	not done	28.5	28.9	17.3	16.2	not done	not done
Loss in mass (g)	128.1	126.3	113.8	114.6	121.3	120.5	124.2	130.7
% loss in mass	91	92.5	80	80	87.5	88	93	94
Observations	black (burnt)	black (burnt)	brown and mouldy	brown and mouldy	brown	brown	black (burnt)	black (burnt)

Results of preliminary tests.

8 The pupils rejected heating over a Bunsen and in an oven at 300°C because the apple lost more than just water.

  a What evidence is there that more than just water was lost?

  b Suggest what else was lost.

9 Suggest <u>two</u> problems of drying the apple at 20°C.

10 These tests didn't show whether chopping up the apple made a difference to the time taken to dry the apple. What extra tests can the class do to find out the answer?

11 In the final plan for their investigation, why did the pupils:

  a chop up the apples;

  b find the mass of the apples on a digital balance;

  c heat in an oven at 100°C;

  d heat to constant mass?

12 Write a list of other ideas that the pupils probably used to make their investigation safe and their results valid.

Controlling variables

In an experiment, lots of things affect the results.
We call these **variables**.

To find out the effect of temperature on dissolving salt, you **vary** the temperature but keep the other things the same. We say that you **control** them. This is to make your test fair.

It makes it easier to spot a pattern in your results if you use a wide **range** for your variable. For example, your results may be too similar to be sure of the pattern if you use only a small range of temperatures.

13 Write down <u>two</u> things that you need to control or keep the same when you investigate the effect of temperature on dissolving.

Selecting equipment

Some choices of equipment are easy but you need to be particularly careful when you choose measuring equipment. Instruments for measuring have a **scale** on them. You need to choose the instrument with a suitable scale for your particular investigation.

For example, measuring the mass of a small strip of magnesium on kitchen scales would not give you a useful reading. A chemical balance would be much more useful. The choice affects the **precision** of your results.

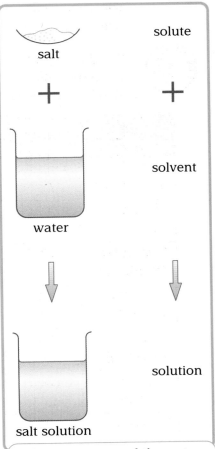

The temperature of the water, the size of the crystals and the amount of stirring all affect the time it takes for the salt to dissolve. These are all variables.

Sean is investigating the force needed to pick up objects in the lab.
He estimates that the weight of these objects varies from 5N to 45N.

14 Choose the best forcemeter for Sean's investigation.
Explain your choice.

Safety

Sometimes you need to use apparatus or chemicals that can be harmful. We call these things **hazards**. You can use them only if you make sure that you and other people are safe. You can look up some hazards in books and others on Hazcards, or you can ask your teacher for help.

Next you need to ask yourself how high a **risk** there is of the hazard causing harm. We call this a **risk assessment**. You do this to decide whether your investigation is safe enough to do. Sometimes the risk assessment helps you to see how to make your investigation safe, for example by wearing eye protection.

15 Where can you find out about possible hazards?

16 What must you do if you are not sure that your investigation is safe enough?

Obtaining and presenting evidence

Before you start an investigation, you need to know exactly:
- what you are going to do;
- what results you are going to record;
- how you are going to record your results, for example in a table on paper or using a datalogger.

Collecting appropriate data

You don't always get the same results from the same experiment. To find out what is really happening, you have to:
- do your experiment several times;
- work out the average result. You find the average by adding together your results and dividing by the number of results. This is sometimes called the **mean**.

Often you can use a range of sources of information and data in an investigation. The more data you have, the easier it is to be confident about your conclusion. A whole class set of results produces even more accurate and reliable data.

17 Why is it more accurate to have several sets of data?

Hazardous chemicals have warning labels. You need to be able to recognise them.

CORROSIVE

This is the sign for an irritant.

This is the sign for a harmful substance.

Presenting results as bar charts or graphs

Often you need to show results in ways that will help you to see any trends and patterns. For example, as a **bar chart** or a **line graph**.

You can use a bar chart to compare one piece of information with another. A line graph shows how a variable changes. You need to choose the best kind of chart or graph for your data as well as a suitable scale for each axis.

Usually when you are plotting a bar chart or a line graph, the variable that you changed goes along the bottom (x-axis) and the one you measured goes up the side (y-axis).

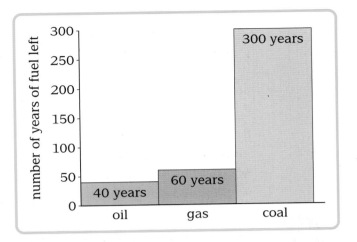

Using computers to collect data and present results

The Internet is a source of information for some investigations. You can also use a computer for **data collection** and **presenting results**.

You can use dataloggers with sensors to record different sorts of environmental changes, for example temperature, amount of light and amount of dissolved oxygen. You can also use them to log the times of readings. So data can be collected over 24 hours without you having to remember to take readings or having to stay up all night.

You can plot the results of experiments, whether collected by hand or with a datalogger, using a spreadsheet program. Careful plotting can make results easier to read. When you get used to using a spreadsheet for plotting graphs, it will also save you time.

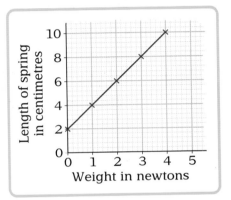

 18 What are the advantages in using a datalogger?

Considering evidence

Identifying trends

Tables, charts and graphs allow you to identify any trends and patterns in your data and to pick out results that do not fit the pattern.

Coming to conclusions

The **conclusion** is where you say what you have found out, so it is an important part of your investigation. You need to describe any trends or patterns and the evidence that supports your conclusion. You should also try to use scientific ideas to explain why you got the results that you did.

Evaluating evidence

Measurement and observation are part of the process of collecting **evidence** to support an explanation or theory. The last part of any investigation is to carry out an **evaluation**. You need to look at the evidence and decide:

- whether there is enough evidence to support a conclusion;
- how you could improve your investigation to increase the strength of your evidence;
- whether or not things presented as evidence are <u>actually evidence</u>.

For example, perhaps you could have:

- taken readings more accurately;
- taken more readings;
- repeated readings.

You also need to try to spot any results that do not fit the general pattern. These are called **anomalous results**.

Look at the graph showing a line of best fit.

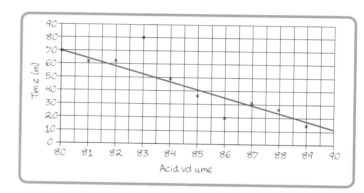

19 Some points on the graph do not lie near the line of best fit. What can you do to improve this set of readings?

Sometimes people give their **opinions**. They may have no evidence for their ideas. Their opinions may be **biased**. They are conclusions that, if correct, would benefit them in some way.

In experimental investigations, you are probably used to evaluating the number and accuracy of readings and know how to deal with readings that don't fit the pattern. You assume that the work of other people who contributed results is accurate and honest. In some other investigations, for example life-style surveys, people don't always tell the truth.

20 a Sometimes smokers deny that they smoke. Suggest reasons.

   b Write down three other life-style or health issues where people sometimes hide the truth.

So, sometimes evidence is gathered inaccurately and sometimes it is incomplete. When your evidence is incomplete, you may find that your explanation turns out to be wrong. This shows just how careful you have to be when you consider and evaluate evidence.

Glossary/Index

Words in *italics* are themselves defined in the glossary.

absorb, absorption   when an *object* or *substance* takes in another object or substance   71, 85, 86, 93–96, 106

acceleration   amount by which *speed* increases in one second; speeding up   138, 144, 146

accurate, accuracy   correct, *precise* and without any mistakes; accurate *evidence* is gathered using accurate measuring instruments with *precision*   60, 84, 102, 106, 129, 130, 163, 166, 168

acid rain   rain that is acidic because it has acidic oxides of sulphur and nitrogen dissolved in it   7

acoustics   how a building *reflects* the sounds produced inside it   106

air   a mixture of *gases*, mainly nitrogen and oxygen 8, 36, 41, 60, 63, 65, 67, 68, 97, 98, 101, 102, 104, 108, 113, 117–119, 136, 141–143, 145, 146, 150, 152

air resistance   the *friction force* acting on an *object* moving through air; also called drag   41, 141, 144, 145

ammeter   *device* used to measure electric *current*   18, 19, 29, 111, 112, 118

ampere, amp (A)   unit of electric *current*   18–20, 24, 27, 29, 112

amplitude   the distance from the centre position of a wave to the peak; the *loudness* of sound   98, 100, 108

anechoic chamber   a room which will *absorb* all sound, with no echoes   106

angle of incidence   the angle between an *incident ray* and the *normal*   87

angle of reflection   the angle between a *reflected ray* and the *normal*   87

anomalous results   results that do not fit the general pattern   168

appliance (electrical)   a *device* that requires an input of electrical energy   26, 27, 111, 113–115, 118

arc   part of a circle   50, 58

area   the measure of the surface of an *object*   49, 147–149, 153, 160

Aristotle   (384–322 BC)   123

armature   a moving *magnetic metal* part of an *electromagnetic device*   80

asteroid belt   rock fragments orbiting the *Sun* between the *orbits* of *Mars* and *Jupiter*   55

astronomer   a scientist who studies the *Sun*, *Moon*, *planets*, *stars* and *Universe*   45, 54–56, 124

atmosphere   the layer of *air* above the *Earth's* surface   54, 57, 129, 143, 154

attract, attraction   two *objects* pulling towards each other   31–33, 44, 72, 73, 77, 80, 81, 119–121, 130

axis   an imaginary line through the centre of the *Earth* about which the Earth spins   45–49, 58

balanced forces   *forces* that are the same size but act in opposite directions   39, 136, 138, 144, 157, 158, 160

bar chart   a way of *presenting results*   6, 102, 103, 167

battery   two or more electrical *cells* joined together   15, 16, 21–24, 26, 28, 29, 82, 110–113, 118

biased, bias   in the case of an *opinion*, based on someone's feelings rather than all the facts   163, 168

biomass energy   a *renewable energy* resource   9, 11

boil, boiling when a *liquid* heats up and turns into a *gas* 60, 61, 64, 67, 70, 71

boiling point the *temperature* at which a *liquid* changes into a *gas* 70, 71

brake a *device* which uses *friction* to stop a vehicle 42, 141, 153

bulb a *device* which *transforms electrical energy* into *light energy* 2, 7, 15–21, 23–25, 29, 65, 66, 82, 111, 115

Bunsen burner a *device* which *burns methane* or *propane* to produce a hot flame 3, 4, 14, 62, 69

Bunsen, Robert (1811–1899) 4

burn, burning when *substances react* with oxygen and release *energy*; also called *combustion* 3, 7, 9, 11, 82, 119, 121, 143

cell (in physics) uses a chemical *reaction* to push an electric *current* around an electric *circuit* 16, 21, 22, 28, 29, 82, 112–113, 118

Celsius a *temperature scale* with the *melting point* of ice written as 0 °C and the *boiling point* of water as 100 °C 60, 71

Celsius, Anders (1701–1744) 60

chemical energy *energy* stored in *fuels* and food 2, 3, 5, 7, 13, 14, 109, 110, 112, 113, 118

circuit (electric) *components* connected together to allow an electric *current* to flow 15–25, 27–29, 80, 81, 111, 112, 116, 118

circuit breaker a *device* which cuts out if too great an electric *current* passes through it 27, 29

circuit symbols a shorthand way of drawing electrical *components* 16

coal a *fossil fuel* 3, 5–7, 109, 117

cochlea part of the inner ear; converts movement into electrical pulses which travel along *nerves* to the brain 104, 107

coil wire wound round and round; used in *electromagnets* 78, 79, 81, 116, 117

compass a *device* which has a *magnetic* needle which points towards the *North Pole* 74–76, 81

components *devices* used in electric *circuits* 15, 16, 18–20, 111, 112, 114, 118

compress, compressed squeeze into a small space 150–152

compressible able to be squeezed into a small space 150, 152, 160

conclusion what you have found out 166–168

condense, condensation when a *gas* cools and changes into a liquid 70, 71

conduction, conduct (i) the flow of an electric *current* through a *substance* (ii) in heat conduction, *energy* passes along a *solid* as its *particles* heat up and *vibrate* faster 62–64, 67, 68, 71

conductor, of electricity will let electricity pass through it 15

conductor, of heat energy will let *heat energy* pass through it 62–64, 71

constellation a group of *stars* that forms a pattern 57, 122, 123, 143

contract become smaller; *solids*, *liquids* and *gases* do this when they cool; *muscles* become shorter and fatter when they contract 60, 156

control the part of an experiment that is needed to make a test fair, where certain *variables* are controlled or kept the same while one variable is varied; it is needed so that we can be sure of the cause of a change or a difference 162, 165

convection a method of heat *transfer* in fluids (*liquids* and *gases*); the fluids at a higher *temperature* rise towards the top of the container they are in 64–68, 71

cooling curve a graph with time on the *x*-axis and *temperature* on the *y*-axis for a *substance* whose temperature is falling 69

Copernicus, Nicolaus (1473–1543) 45, 124

core the centre of an *object*; an *electromagnet* usually has an *iron* core 78–81

current (electric) flows around a complete electric *circuit* 18–25, 27–29, 78–81, 111, 112, 114, 116–118

data information, for example facts or numbers 162–163, 166–167

data collection gathering *data* by any method 167

dawn the time when that part of the *Earth* moves into the *Sun's* light 45, 46

deceleration the amount by which *speed* decreases in one second; slowing down 139, 146

decibel *unit* used to measure the *loudness* of sound 105, 108

Democritus (about 460–370 BC) 123

density, dense the *mass* per *unit volume* of a *substance* 38, 44, 64, 65

device something that changes *energy* from one form into another 10, 15, 16, 109, 111, 118

drag the *friction force* acting on an *object* moving through air or water; also called *air resistance* 41, 44, 142–146

driving force the *force* that makes something move 140, 141

dusk the time when that part of the *Earth* moves out of the *Sun's* light into *shadow* 46

eardrum a tightly stretched skin found at the end of the ear canal; it *vibrates* when sound reaches it 104, 107

Earth the third planet from the *Sun* 32, 33, 45–59, 66, 74, 76, 81, 83, 97, 102, 119–121, 123, 125–130, 143

echolocation a method to judge the distance to *objects*, used by bats; involves sending out a high pitched sound that *reflects* off objects 103, 104

eclipse when bodies line up in space casting one of those bodies into *shadow* 53, 54, 58, 123, 124

efficiency, efficient the fraction, or percentage, of the *energy* supplied that is *transformed* into the desired form of energy 7, 115

effort the size of a *force* applied 158–160

elastic potential energy *energy* stored in things which are stretched or squashed 2, 110

electrical energy the *energy* in wires when electric *current* flows 2, 3, 7, 109–117

electromagnet a *device* which becomes *magnetic* when an electric *current* flows through a wire *coil* 78–81

energy energy is needed to make things happen 1–5, 7–14, 21, 22, 39, 61, 62, 66–70, 82, 97, 98, 105, 109–115, 117–119, 142

engine a machine that uses the *energy* from *fuel* to produce movement 3, 106, 112, 115, 141

evaluation considering whether there is enough *evidence* to support a *conclusion* and whether an investigation can be improved 168

evaporate, evaporation when a *liquid* changes into a gas 8, 70, 71

evidence *observations* and measurements on which *theories* are based 122, 163–164, 166–168

expand, expansion when a *substance* gets bigger because its *particles* speed up and move further apart 60, 150

extension the amount by which something gets longer 34, 44

force a push or a pull 30–36, 39, 41, 42, 44, 99, 119–121, 130, 136, 138, 142–156, 158–160

forcemeter a *device* used to measure the size of a *force* 31, 32, 35, 165

fossil fuels *fuels* formed in the *Earth's* crust from the remains of living things; for example *coal* 5–8, 11, 14, 110, 116–118

frequency the number of waves (for example sound waves) produced every second   99–101, 103, 108

freezing, freeze when a *liquid* cools and becomes *solid*   71

fret part of a guitar, used to reduce the length of string *vibrating*   99

friction a *force* when two surfaces rub past each other; it acts in the opposite direction to the direction in which something is moving   39–42, 44, 77, 136, 139–143, 146

fuel a *substance* that *burns* to release *energy*   2, 3, 6, 7, 9, 11, 14, 117–119, 121, 142

fuse a *device* which *melts* if too great an electric *current* passes through it   27, 29

galaxy a group of millions of *stars*   56–58, 124, 129, 130

Galileo Galilei (1564–1642)   60, 84, 124

Galvani, Luigi (1737–1798)   28

gas a *substance* that spreads out to fill all the space available, but can be *compressed* into a smaller *volume*   4, 51, 63, 64, 68, 70, 71, 102, 108, 150–152, 160

generator machine which *transforms kinetic energy* into *electrical energy*   3, 10, 116–118

geostationary orbit an *orbit* in which a *satellite* stays above the same point on the *Earth's* surface, all the time   127, 128, 130

geothermal energy a *renewable energy* resource   9, 11, 14

Gilbert, William (1544–1603)   76

global warming the heating up of the *Earth* and its *atmosphere*   7

gram (g) *mass* is measured in *units* called grams and *kilograms*; 1000 grams is 1 kilogram   33, 38

gravitational potential energy *energy* stored in *objects* high up   2, 8, 11, 110

gravity, gravitational force, pull the force of *attraction* between two *objects* because of their *mass*   32, 33, 44, 119–121, 125, 126, 130, 136, 138, 144

Hauksbee, Francis (1666–1713)   101

hazards things that are harmful or dangerous and might cause damage   166

heat energy *energy* possessed by hot *objects*; also called *thermal energy*   2, 3, 7, 9–11, 14, 39, 61–71, 115

hemisphere the *Earth* is divided into the northern hemisphere (north of the equator) and the southern hemisphere (south of the equator)   48–50, 123

Herschel, Caroline (1750–1845)   124

Herschel, William (1738–1822)   124

Hertz (Hz) *unit* of *frequency*   99, 103, 108

hydraulic system a system that uses moving *liquid* to work; car *brakes* are an example   153, 160

hydro-electric energy a *renewable energy* resource   8, 11

hypothesis, hypotheses an idea, *theory* or explanation for something, but which has not been tested   161

image the *reflection* of an *object* in a mirror   88, 90, 96

incident ray a beam of light which goes towards an optical *device* such as a mirror or *prism*   87

incompressible cannot be squeezed into a smaller space   152, 160

insulator, insulate, insulation (of *heat energy*) *material* that does not *conduct* heat; it prevents heat loss; (of *electrical energy*) *material* that does not allow an electric *current* to flow   62, 63, 67, 71, 127, 143

iron   a common *metal* element which is a *magnetic material*   28, 31, 72, 73, 75, 76, 78–81, 102

joint   where two bones meet   156

joule (J)   *unit* of *energy* or *work*   1, 4, 12, 14, 61, 67, 71, 113, 114

Jupiter   the fifth *planet* from the *Sun*   33, 55, 120, 124

Kepler, Johannes   (1571–1630)   124

kilocalorie   an alternative *unit* of *energy*, not used much anymore   13

kilogram (kg)   *mass* is measured in *units* called *grams* and kilograms; 1000 grams is 1 kilogram   32, 33, 44, 120, 130

kilojoule   1000 *joules*   12, 13

kilowatts   1000 *watts*   114

kinetic energy   *energy* in a moving *object*   2, 8, 10, 14, 97, 110–112, 115, 116, 118

leap year   a *year* with an extra day; every fourth year   47

Leonardo da Vinci   (1452–1519)   145

lever   used to amplify a *force*; an example is an oar   156–160

light energy   *energy* that *luminous objects* give out   2, 110, 111

light source   anything that produces light; light is *transferred* as *energy* from a light source   82, 83, 96

line graph   a way of *presenting results*   167

liquid   a *substance* that has a fixed *volume* but takes the shape of its container   28, 36, 44, 60, 63–65, 68–71, 102, 108, 152, 153, 160

load   the resistance that a *force* overcomes   158–160

lodestone   a naturally occurring stone which is *magnetic*   72

loudness, loud   the amount of *energy* a sound has; a loud sound has more *energy* than a quiet sound   98, 100, 105–108

loudspeaker   a *device* which converts *electrical energy* into *sound energy*   2, 101, 111

low polar orbit   an *orbit* of a *satellite* close to the *Earth*; the satellite scans the Earth's surface several times a day   128, 130

lubricant   something, usually a *liquid*, that reduces the *friction* between moving parts   39, 40, 44

luminous   gives out its own light   2, 51, 58, 86, 96

lunar   to do with the *Moon*   51–54, 124

lunar month   the amount of time it takes for the *Moon* to *orbit* the *Earth*; 28 days   52, 53

magnet   something which *attracts* a *magnetic material*   31, 72–81, 116, 117, 120

magnetic field   the area around a *magnet* where it exerts a *force* on a *magnetic material*   75, 76, 78, 79, 81, 120

magnetic force   the *force* a *magnet* exerts on a *magnetic material*   72–75, 77, 81

magnetic material   something which will be *attracted* to a *magnet*   72, 73, 75, 78, 81

magnetic tape   used in *devices* such as a cassette recorder to record *data*   77

material   *substances* from which *objects* are made   5, 38, 62, 72, 97, 101, 106, 127, 143

mains electricity   electricity supplied to our homes   26, 29, 110, 114, 116

Mars   the fourth *planet* from the *Sun*   55, 56

mass   the amount of stuff something is made of   32, 33, 37, 38, 44, 120, 121, 125, 130, 163–165

mean   an average; found by adding together a group of results and dividing the total by the number of results   166

melt, melting when a *solid* heats up and changes into a *liquid* 27, 60, 68, 69, 143

melting point the *temperature* at which a *solid* turns into a *liquid* 69, 71

Mercury the nearest *planet* to the *Sun* 55

metals *substances* that *conduct* electricity; they are usually shiny and often hard 35, 62–64, 71, 72, 80, 136

methane a flammable *gas* 3, 4

microphone a *device* which converts sound into electrical signals 100

Milky Way the name of our *galaxy* 56, 124

mineral oil a *fossil fuel* 5–7

molecule the smallest part of a chemical compound and the smallest part of an element that can exist in nature 150–152, 160

moment the turning effect of a *force* 154–160

Moon the natural *satellite* of Earth; other *planets* also have satellite moons, usually lumps of rock 9, 32, 33, 45, 51–54, 56–58, 120–125

muscles tissues and organs that *contract* to cause movement 28, 107, 156

National Grid the network that carries electricity between *power stations* and *substations* 116, 118

natural gas a *fossil fuel* 5–7

Neptune the eighth *planet* from the *Sun* 55, 124

nerves carry electrical impulses around the body 28, 104, 107

Newton, Isaac (1642–1727) 32, 33, 91, 92, 120, 151

newton (N) the *unit* of *force* 31–37, 44, 120, 130, 142, 147–148, 151–153, 156, 157, 160

noise pollution too much unwanted sound 106, 108

non-luminous does not give out its own light 51, 58, 86, 96

non-metal elements that are not *metals* 71, 72

non-magnetic materials 72, 73, 81

non-renewable a *fuel* which cannot be used again 6, 8, 9, 14

normal a line drawn at 90° to the point where a *ray of light* hits a mirror or a *prism* 87, 89, 90, 96

north-seeking pole the end of a *magnet* which if left to spin freely will point towards the *Earth's North Pole* 74, 81

nuclear fuels *fuels*, such as uranium, used in nuclear *power stations* 116, 117

nuclear radiation *energy* given out in nuclear *reactions* 7, 117

nuclear reactors where *nuclear fuel reacts* to give *heat energy* 7

observations records of changes, similarities, differences and other features 122, 163, 168

object something which if placed in front of a mirror will form an *image* on the other side of the mirror 2, 32, 33, 36, 37, 88, 96, 110, 118–121, 130, 137, 139, 141, 142, 146, 160

opaque will not allow light to pass through it 86, 96

opinion what someone thinks – but not supported by conclusive *evidence* 163, 168

orbit, orbiting the path of a *satellite* around a *planet* or of a planet around a *star* 45, 47, 51–56, 58, 124–130

oscilloscope a *device* which shows a picture of a wave which represents a sound wave 100, 108

parallel circuit an electric *circuit* in which there are two or more different routes for the electric *current* 23–25, 29, 112

particle   a very small piece of matter that everything is made of   62–65, 68–70, 77, 97, 98, 99, 101, 102, 143

pascal (Pa)   *unit* of *pressure*   149, 160

periscope   a *device*, made from two mirrors, which can be used to see over walls or from submarines which are under water   88

petrol   a *fuel* which can be burnt in a car *engine*   3, 41, 141–143

phases (of the Moon)   the different stages in the appearance of the *Moon* every *lunar month*   51, 52, 58

Philolaus   (5th century BC)   123

pitch   how high or low sound is   98–100, 103, 108

pivot   the point around which something turns, or tries to turn   154–160

planet   a body that *orbits* a *star*   33, 50, 51, 54–58, 120, 122–126, 130

Pluto   the ninth *planet* from the *Sun*   55, 124

pneumatic   the action of machines that use gas *pressure* to work; a pneumatic drill is an example   150, 160

Pole, North   the most northerly point of the *Earth's* axis   45

Pole, South   the most southerly point of the *Earth's* axis   45

Pole Star   the *star* directly above the *North Pole*   57, 123

pollution   contamination of the environment with unwanted *materials* or *energy*   7, 8, 10, 11, 14

potential difference   what makes an electric *current* flow round a *circuit*; another word for *voltage*   112, 118

potential energy   the energy that is stored in something because it is high up (*gravitational*) or because it is bent or stretched (*elastic*)   110, 118

power station   where electricity is generated by *burning fuels*   3, 7, 116–118

power supply   pushes the electric *current* around an electric *circuit*   18, 25

precision, precise   *accuracy* of measurements and measuring instruments   163, 165

predict, prediction   to say what you think will happen   122, 123, 162

preliminary tests   tests, trial runs and information searches carried out to find out the best approach to an investigation   164

presenting results   showing results in a way that makes them easy to read and understand   167

pressure   how much pushing *force* there is on an *area*   147–155, 160

primary colours   red, green and blue are the primary colours of light   94

prism   a device, made of glass or plastic, which *refracts* light twice, it can be used to produce a *spectrum*   91–93, 97

propane   a flammable *gas*   3, 4

proportional   two quantities whose values increase at the same rate are proportional to each other   34, 44

Ptolemy   (about AD 90–168)   123, 124

pylon   structures that support the overhead electrical cables that are part of the *National Grid*   113, 116

quadrat   an *object*, often a square frame, used for sampling living things   162

radiation (of heat)   a method of heat *transfer*, where the *heat energy* is given out as infra-red waves   66, 68, 71

random   by chance; random movement is in a direction that cannot be *predicted*   150, 162

range   the values between the lowest and the highest value fall within the range   31, 60, 103, 165

vacuum an empty space with nothing inside, not even *air* 68, 101, 108

validity, of results whether results are *accurate*, measuring instruments are *precise* and used properly 163

variable in an experiment, something that can be changed to affect the result 162, 165, 167

variable resistor a *resistor* whose value can be changed 20, 29

variations, vary differences; to differ; to change something 162, 165

Venus the second *planet* from the *Sun* 55

vibrate, vibration a constant backwards and forwards motion 62, 97–102, 104–108

volt (V) the *unit* of *voltage* 21, 28, 29

Volta, Alessandro (1818–1889) 28, 29

voltage a measure of the amount of *energy* supplied to an electric *circuit* 21, 24–27, 78, 112–114, 116, 118

voltmeter *device* used to measure *voltage* 112, 118

volume the amount of space that something takes up; it is measured in cubic centimetres (cm^3) or millilitres (ml) 38, 44, 150, 151, 152, 160

watt (W) *unit* of power; there are 1000 watts in a *kilowatt* (kW) 114

wave energy a *renewable energy* resource 8, 11

weight the *force* of *gravity* on a *mass*; measured in *newtons* 32, 33, 36, 37, 44, 120, 121, 127, 130, 144, 150, 154, 157–158, 160, 165

wind energy a *renewable energy* resource 8, 10, 14

work change in *energy* 1

year the time for a *planet* to complete one *orbit* of its *star* 47, 48, 55, 56, 122, 123, 126, 130

Acknowledgements

We are grateful to the following for permission to reproduce photographs:

ArenaPAL.com 107 (Clive Barda); **Art Directors and Trip Photo Library** 128 (NASA), 158b (Roger Chester); **Paul Beard Photo Agency** 139, (Matthew Nobel); **Bubbles Photolibrary** 12l (Jennie Woodcock), 12tr (Angela Hampton), 12br (Chris Rout); **Trevor Clifford** 99tr, 99m, 99b, 100; **Corbis** 111mr, 113 (Charles Mauzy), 132t, 132br, 132bl (Tom Brakefield), 133 (Philippe Giraud), 158m (Charles O'Rear); **Empics Sports Photo Agency** 141 (Neil Simpson); **Fisher Scientific** 167; **Getty Images** 123t (Jeremy Walker); **Philip Harris Education** 31, 111l (t-b); **HMSO** 43; **Istituto e Museo di Storia della Scienza** (Franca Principe) 60cr; **ISVR Consulting** 106t; **Nigel Luckhurst** 70; **Jean Martin** 162; **Vanessa Miles** 42, 73m, 103b, 111tr, 111br, 114t, 114b, 132cr, 154; **Natural History Photographic Agency** 5 (Daniel Heuclin), 103t (Manfred Danegger), 104t (Alan Williams); **Nature Picture Library** 104bl (Artur Tabor), 104br (Duncan McEwan), 161 (Tony Heald); **Redferns** 99tl (Geoff Dann), 106m (Mick Hutson); **Science and Society** 6 (NMPFT); **Science Photo Library** 1l (David Ducros), 1c (Jim Selby), 1tr (Alan and Sandy Carey), 1br (Simon Fraser), 3 (l-r) (Deep Light Productions, David Nunuk, Alan Sirulnikoff, Martin Bond), 7 (Mark Clarke), 12c (Simon Fraser), 13 (David Frazier/Agstock), 32 (Hank Morgan/Geosphere Project), 46 (Pekka Parviainen), 51 (John Sandford), 53 (Dr Fred Espenak), 54t (Dr Fred Espenak), 54c (David Nanuk), 54b (New York Public Library), 56t (NASA), 56b (Julian Baum), 57 (SPL), 60tl (Astrid and Hanns-Frieder Michler), 60tr (Chris Priest and Mark Clarke), 65 (Marty F. Chillmaid), 77 (Martin Bond), 92 (David Parker), 102 (Keith Kent), 116t (Sheila Terry), 116b (Martin Bond), 129t (Space Telescope Science Institute), 158t (Maximilian Stock Ltd); **John Walmsley** 98, 106b; **Elizabeth Whiting Associates** 109 (Tim Street-Porter).

Picture research: Vanessa Miles and Jacqui Rivers

We have made every effort to trace copyright holders, but if we have inadvertently overlooked any we will be pleased to make the necessary arrangements at the earliest opportunity.